Brother André

of

Saint Joseph's Oratory

By

William H. Gregory

WILLIAM J. HIRTEN CO., INC.
25 Barclay Street—New York
1925

THE KNICKERBOCKER PRESS, NEW ROCHELLE, N. Y.

BROTHER ANDRÉ

Dedicated to My Beloved Wife

Bessie C. Gregory

whose devotion inspired this narrative

Foreword

ANNUALLY thousands of Americans visiting Canada are confused concerning the great Oratory of St. Joseph on the flank of Mount Royal. They hear many fantastic tales woven about the shrine and that humble, pious religious, Brother André whose devotion has made it possible.

The amount of misinformation disseminated concerning Brother André perplexed me on my first visit. I mentioned the fact to a priest friend in Montreal. He explained that he heard the same complaint hundreds of times during the season and suggested that I prepare this brochure especially for the American pilgrims. It is estimated that 300,000 Americans visited the shrine during 1924.

If this narrative aids American tourists, especially those not of the Catholic faith, in better understanding the great work being carried on at this citadel of faith I shall feel that my effort has not been in vain.

I hereby gratefully acknowledge the aid

and encouragement given me by Brother André and the priests at St. Joseph's Oratory in preparation of this work. The photographs herein contained are reproduced through the courtesy of the Canadian Pacific Railway.

W. H. G.

Contents

CHAPTER   PAGE

I.—Brother André   1

II.—The Oratory   57

III.—The Pilgrims   68

IV.—What Is a Miracle ?   .   .   .   101

V.—Cures   107

Illustrations

FACING
PAGE

BROTHER ANDRÉ . . . . *Frontispiece*

THE SHRINE CHAPEL TWENTY YEARS AGO . 34

THE CRYPT AT SAINT JOSEPH'S ORATORY . 50

A LARGE PILGRIMAGE AT THE ORATORY . 66

CRUTCHES OF SUFFERERS LEFT AT THE ORATORY 82

THE BASILICA WHEN COMPLETED . . . 114

I

𝕭𝖗𝖔𝖙𝖍𝖊𝖗 𝕬𝖓𝖉𝖗𝖊

A GREAT living torrent of suffering continuously sweeps toward the rocky slopes of Mount Royal, in Montreal, where the great Oratory of Saint Joseph towers high above the cliffs, a mighty beacon of hope for suffering humanity.

Faith, there, is a living, throbbing thing proclaiming in thunderous tones the mercy, goodness and might of Heaven in answering the prayers and appeals of the afflicted. The flotsam and jetsam of this world of suffering eagerly struggle into the mighty floodtide of faith and devotion that whirls about this, the greatest shrine in honor of the Protector of the Holy Family in the World.

From their couches of misery all over the North American continent these afflicted clients of Saint Joseph, suffering from every form of distress and withstanding indescribable hardships to make the journey, come that they may prostrate themselves before the

1

shrine of the powerful patron and implore his intervention for the alleviation of their ills. The conviction of the devout pilgrims that these rugged cliffs have been especially selected for supernatural manifestations of the power and goodness of the patron seem well founded as this narrative will reveal. That remarkable cures have taken place in cases long abandoned by medical science as incurable is no longer seriously challenged even by those whose great passion seems to be hatred of all religion and especially anything even remotely connected with the Roman Catholic Church.

Many of these cures have been authenticated by distinguished physicians and surgeons not of the Catholic faith. While the authenticated records of many remarkable recoveries from disease that cannot be accounted for by science have been carefully preserved it might be well to explain here that they have never been presented to an ecclesiastical tribunal for determination nor explanation. If special graces have been showered down on the faithful through intercession to Saint Joseph at the Oratory, the Church has thus far failed to officially recognize them. The events have been unofficially investigated but the Church has never claimed, admitted nor denied that

supernatural manifestations have taken place
in this citadel of Faith within the metropolis
of Canada.

However, the fact that the Catholic Church
has not officially proclaimed the cures and
graces as miracles has not deterred the faithful in Canada and the United States who are
familiar with the extraordinary happenings,
from pronouncing their judgment that Saint
Joseph has chosen the rugged hillside of Mount
Royal as a special place on earth for supernatural manifestations.

The Oratory, today, as a place of pilgrimage although it was only started within
this generation surpasses the world famed
Grotto at Lourdes, France, where the Blessed
Virgin appeared to Bernadette, for the number
of supplicants annually attracted to it. The
amazing growth of this shrine, from obscurity to the world's greatest place of pilgrimage within such a short span of years,
without any organized propaganda or publicity, has been remarkable. Many have wondered at the astounding growth of this center
of devotion to the Head of the Holy Family
and this narrative is designed to reveal just
why the Oratory has taken its place as the
foremost shrine in the world.

The tourist on reaching Montreal quickly

gets some explanation of the rise of the Oratory. He hears fascinating tales that have been woven about that humble, pious, saintly old apostle of faith, Brother André, whose great passion-like devotion to Saint Joseph has made the shrine possible. The aged Brother is pictured as a sort of a wonder worker, a miracle man, a worldly dispenser of heavenly blessings who is endowed with supernatural powers to cure all earthly ills. An effort is made to throw an air of mystery about the pious old religious. This is done by those who depend on tourists for their living and is designed to excite the interest of persons visiting Montreal who might not otherwise visit the shrine. The vast majority of the yarns thus circulated are entirely without foundation but this does not deter the commercial interests that annually reap a harvest from the pilgrims by disseminating them.

A Citadel of Faith

Saint Joseph's Oratory is without doubt the most unique and extraordinary shrine in the world. Although more Roman Catholics are attracted to it annually than visit any similar center of devotion, numbered among the hosts that daily visit it are many thousands of Protestants and Jews. The earnestness of these non-Catholic pilgrims and their intimate knowledge of the shrine is impressive. In fact, their sincerity and reverence at times seems even greater than that of Catholics who all their lives have been familiar with the great devotions of the church. The ardent faith of these has often been rewarded in extraordinary ways.

The devotion of the Catholics to Saint Joseph is easily understood. Through the ages he has been placed in an exalted position by the Church. That a great Basilica in his honor should be erected in a country that for centuries has been under his patronage seemed fitting and proper. However, the fact that the Oratory which is certainly destined to become the world's foremost shrine should be conceived and made possible only through the burning faith of a humble Brother of the Congregation of the Holy Cross and that extraordinary cures of undoubted supernatural origin have taken place on the rugged cliffs of Mount Royal greatly increases the interest of thousands in the man and his work. To secure accurate information concerning this pious old apostle of faith whose eyes ever burn with the light of unextinguishable love for his patron, proved a most difficult task even for one trained in the methods and ways of American journalism.

In the beginning the effort seemed almost hopeless because of the many confusing and sometimes ridiculous stories that have been woven about Brother André. In the first place the majority of the pilgrims and those who know the "Saint of Mount Royal" the best are French Canadians, an extremely religious and imaginative people. To them Brother André is a saint on earth, a chosen representative of Saint Joseph. Toward him they display the same respect they reserve for the Divine. Any scrap of fantastic tale they hear concerning this holy man, no matter how weird or ridiculous it may sound in the telling, they eagerly grasp and without apparent difficulty convince themselves of its authenticity. In hushed tones and with real sincerity they repeat these stories to tourists and pilgrims, picturing Brother André as a superman, a great "Faith Doctor" who can perform miracles at will and cure all bodily afflictions simply by willing them cured. Many of the tales are silly. They have not only proven embarrassing to Brother André and his co-workers at the Oratory but have seriously tended to reflect on and obstruct the work being carried on there.

Fantastic Tales

One of the most widely circulated of these stories which is heard not only in Canada but in the United States deals with an alleged conflict between Brother André and certain of the ecclesiastical authorities who were supposed to have attempted to curb his activities. According to one version of the story, a high church dignitary called on Brother André, denounced his practice of receiving pilgrims and demanded that he immediately cease conferring with them and return to his humble tasks as porter and man of all work in the Holy Cross order. When this demand was made, the story continues, Brother André, to defeat the aims of his superior who is pictured as being inspired by jealousy, by use of the supernatural power he is supposed to be endowed with, forced his visitor to grant him permission to continue his work. This story is entirely without foundation. It has been so widely spread that it has greatly embarrassed Brother André and the other alleged participants in the incident. Insidious yarns of this character spread like wild fire and tend to confuse and mislead the public on the objects and work being carried on at the Oratory. The situation is extremely unfortunate in that these baseless stories lead to unjust and uncalled-for criticism of the Oratory and those who through it are giving their lives to spreading devotion to the head of the Holy Family. These foolish stories are also pounced upon by anti-religionists who are ever anxious to thunder their contempt for anything even remotely connected with religion and put it in a false and ridiculous light before the world.

As may be gleaned from the foregoing, considerable difficulty was encountered in learning the truth concerning the origin, life and work of the "Saint of Mount Royal." The facts on which this narrative is based were obtained during a long and exhaustive interview with Brother André. When the venerable religious learned that the data concerning him was especially sought for presentation to the American people, in his pious, humble way he declared that he would do anything in his power for the people of the United States. His deep regard for Americans and things American seems to be one of his outstanding characteristics. He speaks English haltingly and with the greatest difficulty. Frequently after pondering over just what he wants to say and failing to find in his limited English vocabulary the proper words or expression to convey his idea he will substitute his native French.

His Nativity

The man whom the world knows, honors and respects as Brother André first saw the light of day on August 9, 1845, at Saint Gregoire d'Iberville, in the Province of Quebec, Canada. He was baptized Alfred Bessette, being the sixth son of Isaac and Clothilde Foisy Bessette, the parents of eleven children. Life for two of the children was moth winged, too frail for a sturdy world, and they passed away in infancy.

Isaac Bessette was a poverty stricken, loyal and deeply religious French-Canadian. He was known throughout the sparsely settled neighborhood as an industrious, skilled but unfortunate toiler. His source of income was derived from his trade which was the same as that of Saint Joseph, a wheelwright and joiner. This trade during the period when he was struggling to care for his young family was surely not a profitable one. In fact, there was little or nothing for carriage makers to do in the district. Frequently those who followed the trade were forced to hire themselves out as laborers in the surrounding country. Isaac Bessette was in this class and spent more time laboring in the fields and woods than he did at his chosen calling.

The home of the family at the time of the birth of Alfred was little more than a frontier shack. It was in the town but still in the woods and giants of the forest towered over it. The house was fairly well constructed considering the facilities available for such work at the time. The hewn logs that were used in the walls came from the nearby forest. They were well fitted on the ends and the cracks between them were packed with clay. The living quarters were cramped considering the size of the family and barely sufficient for its wants. The only decoration inside the ill lighted home of the Bessettes was a large crucifix that hung from a peg in the wall.

The life of the family was simple. Those who were old enough worked hard all day. There was no recreation except work. An important feature in the daily routine of the family was the recitation aloud of the morning and evening prayers in unison. They saw little of their neighbors except on Sunday when they gathered for Mass in the little frontier chapel.

About five years after the birth of Alfred the Bessette family moved to Farnham,

Quebec, in hope that the better opportunities offered by this community would improve their condition. It was a hope never realized. For the following four years Isaac Bessette continued the bitter struggle to earn enough to supply his family with the bare necessities of life. Instead of improving, conditions seem to have become worse and then came the great tragedy. Isaac Bessette died leaving an almost penniless widow with nine little children to care for. The Spartan widow vainly sought a solution of the gigantic problem that confronted her. The hardy, kindly people of the frontier came to her aid as best they could but they had little to offer. The task of keeping the children together proved hopeless and she was forced to scatter them among relatives for upbringing.

A Frail Youth

Alfred always frail, timid and sickly was sent off to the home of an uncle, M. Timothee Nadeau of St. Cesaire de Rouville. He was the one the Widow Bessette worried about the most because of his continuous ill health. He lived with his uncle until he was fifteen years old.

The dark days of poverty when his parents were making their almost hopeless fight for

existence had left their indelible mark on
the orphan boy. He was unable to attend
the village school long enough to grasp even
the rudiments of learning. He would go with
some degree of regularity for a week or so
and then the strain would prove too much
for him and he would be forced to remain away
from school for a long period. His uncle, not
oversupplied with this world's goods, was
forced to work hard on his farm to support
his family. He had no time for the instruc-
tion of the weak orphan boy although he did
display a real fatherly interest in him. The
boy was too frail to assist in any of the many
pressing duties about the farm. His life was
uneventful except for the various periods of
sickness that he survived.

When Alfred was twelve years old he was
struck a crushing blow by the death of his
mother. He had loved her very dearly and had
often dreamed of the day when she would once
more gather her scattered family together and
they would all be so happy. The child mind
did not grasp the significance of her death.
His uncle explained it all to him as gently as
he could. After this Alfred was very sad and
mourned much. Often long after the rest of
the household was asleep the orphan boy was
still on his knees in the chilled room offering

up hundreds of "Aves" for his mother. His
great hope of being of service to her on earth
was shattered but he never forgot her in his
prayers.

In speaking of this period in his life Brother
André said:

I was never very strong. From the time when
I was a little boy, ten years old I have suffered
from dyspepsia. It seems as if I was always sick
from it. I have had it all during my life and it
still annoys me.

When I was living with my uncle and was very
young I could not go to school much because I
was always sick. Once I tried to become a shoemaker but I could not stand bending over and
being inside the place so much and my health
made me give it up. Then after a little while
when I thought I was strong enough I tried to become a baker but again I found that my health
would not let me do inside work. It seems that
I was never very strong.

The simple life on the farm in his early
boyhood had not revealed much of the world
to the orphan boy. While living with his
uncle he became of age to go to church. Then
on Sunday he was taken with the rest of the
family to Mass. He soon learned that the
black-robed priest was the most important

man in the community and that, in fact, the church was the most important part of the whole community. He met other boys of his own age after Mass and with them stood nearby while the gossip and news of the neighborhood was disseminated following the service. He listened intently to all that was said and he heard many wonderful things that caused him to dream of the world beyond the great woods.

Picturesque Natives

As the faithful poured out of the backwoods church and gathered in little groups to discuss the sermon and the events of the week they presented a strange and interesting picture. They were garbed for the most part in rough homespun. The men wore heavy coats with wide collars to protect them from the icy blasts that swept down from the North woods. Some of the coats were fur lined as were their caps. The clothes of the women were made more for service and protection than for style. Many of them following the custom of their native country covered their heads with shawls rather than hats. Among the groups here and there were brilliant flashes of color revealing pretty sashes or shawls that made their owners envied by

their less fortunate neighbors. Some of the
women wore beautiful fur coats made of
rare pelts. The clothes of the children were
much like those of their elders and had the
appearance of having been "cut down" to
fit them.

A Wondrous Tale

Once young Bessette was so fortunate as
to get a place near the priest while the latter
was listening to a tale of the experiences of
one of the young woodsmen who had traveled far into the United States to work in the
winter. This young man was the center of
an admiring circle and well might he be. Had
he not completed a great journey? Look at
the fine coat he wore and the bright colors of
his other garments.

The sturdy young woodsman was telling
of the great empire to the south. He pictured
it as a wonderful land of opportunity, a land
of plenty where high wages were paid and
where conditions were ideal in every way.
He said that the driving blizzards of the
bleak north were unknown there. They had
snow, to be sure, but the storms lacked the
fury and intensity of those at home. Winter
far below the great river was not a time to be
spent in fighting the elements for fear of per-

ishing. There men worked at their appointed
tasks and received in pay as much for a
week's labor as they did in Canada for a
month's hard work.

Excited questions were hurled at the trav-
eler from all sides. He answered them gladly
in simple language. Then the smiling priest
interposed an inquiry. He wanted to know
had the young man missed Mass while he
was away and was delighted to find out that
he had not. He explained with great detail
that near the factory where he worked in
New England there was a little Catholic
Church and that many of the communicants
were French-Canadians. The young men
seemed greatly interested in what they had
heard. They loitered about exchanging scraps
of news, but the conversation always reverted
to the wonderful land to the south, the
United States.

When they were returning from Mass
that day Alfred heard his uncle repeat the
story as related by the young man to the
women folks who had not heard it, almost
word for word as he told it. He was much
impressed. After that he often dreamed of
the land of plenty where men were paid such
high wages.

His great concern had always been to im-

prove his health to a point where he could
take his place with the great army of sturdy
empire builders in the north who were push-
ing the frontier of civilization into the Canadian wilderness.   Now, he reasoned if he could
become strong enough to work he might
journey to the United States. With this in
mind he hired himself out as a day laborer
to the farmers in the vicinity of Saint Cesaire.
He gave everything he had to his work but
the expected and much hoped for improvement in health failed to materialize. He
shifted about the countryside from one farm
to another attracting little or no attention
because his frail frame was unequal to the
rough hard work laborers such as he were
called on and expected to do. He often heard
men boast of deeds of great strength and
wondered if he ever would be able to dupli-
cate their feats.

It was while he was thus engaged as a
laborer that he first came to the special attention of the Rev. M. Springer, the curé at
Farnham who was so instrumental in discov-
ering he had a vocation. The kindly priest
took a friendly interest in the earnest, timid
farm hand from the time he met him. He
asked him to call at the rectory and discuss
his problems promising to give what aid he

could in their solution. Alfred Bessette poured out the story of his life to his black-robed friend. The priest listened patiently and with great sympathy. He appreciated the struggle the youth was making and breathed into his ear words of encouragement. Their friendship grew and young Bessette became a frequent caller at the rectory.

One farmer after another failed to keep him in his employ because of his inability to do his share of the work. Finally when he was unable to find work the priest took him into his household as a chore boy. This was really the turning point in the career of the future founder of the shrine that now annually attracts over half a million people to Montreal.

To New England

Just how long Brother André remained in the employ of Father Springer he does not recall. It was not for a great period, however. While he was thus engaged he was seized with a great desire to better himself in the world. He heard more tales of the great opportunities in the United States from French-Canadians who came home. The ambition that had been smouldering in his breast, since first he heard the wondrous tales of America, was again fired. He decided to offer himself to American employers at the first opportunity. He told many of his desire and a friend who had worked in Connecticut and was returning to that state promised to find him employment and to send for him. Soon after this man returned to the United States he communicated with the chore boy and told him that a job was waiting for him at a cotton mill near Plainfield, Conn.

Brother André does not recall the exact location of the mill where he first worked as a general laborer nor does he recall the name of the man who operated it. He worked at the mill but a short time when his body was again racked by the old ailments that had always forced him to seek work in the outdoors. He was forced to give up the position for fear of a complete breakdown. This was indeed a serious step for the youth to take because it left him without any means of support in a strange land. He did not hesitate long as to what course he would follow. He immediately sought employment as a farm handy man or man of all work. The strength that he hoped would come to him in the milder climate did not materialize. He quickly obtained work for labor was scarce, but did not last at it long. He was a struggling weakling thrown among the people of a hardy race who had little time or money to waste on him. He was utterly unequal to the tasks set out for him by the various farmers that employed him. His Spartan soul refused to allow him to admit defeat and for three years he went from farm to farm in New England giving the best he had which was not good enough to hold any job long.

The time that Brother André spent in New England although the work was hard and the compensation did not come up to his expectations was, however, a very happy period in his life. Frequently in his travels about the countryside either at work or looking for work he met French-Canadians who had invaded America on a mission similar to his. Through the aid of friendly countrymen who could read and write he managed to keep in fairly constant communication with his old pastor and friend at Saint Cesaire. He told the priest of his almost futile attempt to establish himself in America and revealed to him his hopes and his dreams for the future. The answers came back promptly bringing him messages of courage and hope from his native land.

The youthful Alfred Bessette grew to love those New England hills where he labored so hard. And he still retains that love now when he is well advanced in years and the strain of his work is heavy on him. Twice a year he leaves the great Oratory on the back of Mount Royal and takes vacations among the lonely hills and valleys where as a youth he sought in vain to establish himself. On these trips to New England his whereabouts is carefully guarded and he roams about without attracting any attention and returns to his life work always better for the visit.

At the age of twenty-three Alfred Bessette became convinced that America did not hold much promise of a future for him. He returned to his native land and took up his residence with relatives at Sutton, Quebec. While there he had an opportunity to make frequent visits to his old pastor. Their friendship had grown very close. One night while they were alone in the rectory young Bessette unfolded to the priest the secret of his heart. He declared that since his early youth when he had served at Mass his great desire had been to enter the service of his Maker. He told of his great devotion to the head of the Holy Family, and said that it was his most ardent hope that in some way no matter how small he might be the means of spreading further devotion to his patron, Saint Joseph.

The priest listened patiently to this son of the soil, uneducated and sickly, voice his desire to enter the service of God. At the same time he realized his utter unfitness for the work he hoped to undertake and his heart was filled with sympathy for the young man. Before him sat an earnest, sincere, God-loving and God-fearing youth filled with ambition for the life of a religious. It seemed that the possibility of the fulfillment of his hope was remote, if not hopeless. He could not read or write and had not even the rudiments of education. The priest was patient and careful in his conversation after hearing of the ambitions of the farmer boy who had failed because of his weak constitution.

It was the sincere passion-like devotion of this great apostle of faith to Saint Joseph who sat before the priest that prompted the latter to withhold judgment on his qualifications and promise to do everything within his power to further his ambition. His faith was a marvelous thing to behold. It was the faith of a strong character with strong, sound convictions. It was more than faith, it was life itself to him. Within him there seemed to

burn the same faith that gave the Holy
Martyrs strength and courage to suffer persecution, torture and death in its cruelest
forms, smilingly for Christianity. The eyes
of the humble youth blazed and he made
no attempt to disguise his feelings on the
subject.

In speaking of his devotion to Saint Joseph
with the writer he said:

"I think that my devotion to Saint Joseph was
born while I was but a little boy at Saint Cesaire.
The pastor there had great devotion to Saint
Joseph. He was a very devout man but especially
so when he was talking of the head of the Holy
Family. There, as everywhere throughout the
civilized world, the month of March is set aside
by the Catholic Church for special devotion to
Saint Joseph.

"The good 'Curé' taught me the simple little
prayers to say in his honor during the month of
March. He also taught me something of the life
of Saint Joseph. I was much impressed by the
prayers and also by the absolute confidence the
pastor had in the patron of all Canada. I think
it was this great confidence of the priest that
kindled in my heart the first sparks of love for
Saint Joseph. However, now it seems as if I had
always prayed to the mighty saint who has been so
good to all people who have sought his aid. The
world would be better and there would be more

happiness if more people would recommend themselves to him."

His Vocation

As soon as Alfred Bessette made known
his desire to dedicate his life to the service of
God he became the subject of careful inquiry
by his pastor. Kindly, through skillful in-
terrogation and keen observation, the priest
ascertained that his youthful friend had a
real vocation. He questioned him at length
on many subjects and soon learned that his
real passion in life was his devotion to his
patron. The sincere, pious laborer who
sought to give his life to the service of God
and his patron was an object of pity in the
eyes of his pastor. If he could read and
write there might have seemed to be some
hope. He might study at home until he was
ready to enter high school or college, but with
his terrible handicap it all seemed hopeless.

Coupled with this condition, was the fact
that he was sickly, which seemed to shut
him off forever from the goal he sought to
attain, the priesthood. However, the facts
as stated above did not deter the good priest
from retaining his interest and breathing
words of encouragement into the ears of the
applicant, for service in the work of God. He

pondered over the problem for some time and sought to ascertain where he might place the youth in a religious order which might be able to use someone of his type. In his quest he was extremely fortunate.

A short time before Alfred Bessette made known his desire to enter the service of God, the religious of the Congregation of the Holy Cross started the organization of a commercial college in the parish. This naturally brought the members of the great teaching Order in close contact with the local pastor. He soon told them of the young man of the parish who was anxious to embark on a religious career. He frankly revealed the applicant's lack of education, but impressed on them his many sterling qualities at the same time professing the belief that he had a vocation. He recommended that they at least grant him a personal interview wherein they might ascertain for themselves the facts he had conveyed to them. They were busy with their work of organization and at first were reluctant to even talk with young Bessette. In great detail they explained to the pastor that a thorough education was essential to anyone joining a teaching Order such as theirs. However, their arguments did not sway the priest and he urged that they talk with the

young man and accept him if possible. To
please the priest more than anything else
the Brothers finally consented to talk with
him.

Alfred Bessette was thrilled when he heard
of the coming interview. He devoted himself
to prayer for days before it, asking the aid
and guidance of his patron. The great day
arrived and he was ushered into the presence
of two of the Brothers. They received him in
a kindly way and immediately put him at
ease. He felt that he was talking with friends
who understood him and appreciated his
desires.

The interview took place in the plain, simple
parlor of a backwoods rectory. Although the
participants at the time, of course, had no
reason to suspect it, their meeting symbolized
the entry into the service of God, of one
of the most unique and influential religious
characters of the century.

The Brothers who were deputized to represent the Congregation in the conference
took part with a feeling akin to deep sympathy for the postulant who was about to
offer his life in the service of the community.
They knew well that he was ill fitted for the
work he sought to take up. They felt sorry for
him but were careful not to reveal their feel-

ings. They asked him why he wished to enter their Order and whether he thought he had a vocation.

In simple language the applicant told his story. Its very simplicity made it impressive. It revealed his humble nature and his intense passion-like devotion to his patron. His auditors pointed out that his ill-health and utter lack of education certainly failed to fit him for service in a body of men who devoted their lives to teaching. He agreed with them that he could not be used as an instructor but begged an opportunity to be of some service. He said he would be willing to perform any task assigned to him no matter how humble if he were admitted to the community. He continued his pleas for admission to the Order for some time and finally the Brothers gave him a promise that they would consult their superiors and recommend him to them.

The Humble Novice

In 1870, Alfred Bessette was admitted to the Novitiate of the Congregation of the Holy Cross at Saint Laurant. After taking his preliminary vows he was given the name of Frère André (Brother André). The youthful novice found himself in the company of highly intelligent men who lived with Spartan simplicity within the wall of their gray and mossy establishment. He quickly learned that these fasting, praying, hard working men about him had a really great mission in life, that of the education of the youth of the country. He further learned that it is possible for piety and joyousness to exist at one and the same time within one and the same person. He also discovered that a long, gloomy face was not essential to a religious. The men he was thrown in contact with were certainly happy in their work.

The youthful novice was assigned to many hard tasks. He washed dishes and waited on the table while the others ate. Then after taking his own slender meal, part of his work included scrubbing the floors and later helping with the mending of the clothes of the active field workers of the community. His smiling humility and great desire for work in the service of his Maker soon made him a favorite in the community. For a whole year the novice was a dishwasher and general handy man. In that time he convinced his superiors of his worth and of the fact that he had a real vocation. They decided he would make a very desirable member of the Order and after the beginning of the second year when he had renewed his vows he was

given his first assignment. He was sent to
the College of Notre Dame, at Cotes Des
Neiges, Montreal, as a porter.

This old institution of learning situated at
the foot of the western slopes of Mount Royal
is maintained by the Congregation of the
Holy Cross exclusively for the education of
boys between the ages of seven and twelve.
The school is famous throughout Canada for
the excellence of its teaching staff and the
number of distinguished Canadian profes-
sional and business men who have received
their elementary training there.

The Doorkeeper

When Brother André first reported to his
superior the post of doorkeeper and general
messenger was vacant. He seemed just the
man for the position because he could not
teach. The assignment required that he
answer the door bell, ascertain the mission of
the caller and then summons the individual
sought. Surely the assignment was not an
important one, but Brother André liked it and
declares that he was very happy during the
period he spent as doorkeeper. Now, in re-
ferring to it he always humorously explains
that he had hardly finished his novitiate
before his superiors "showed him the door"

and that he "remained there for forty years —without leaving."

The new doorkeeper with his polite, gentle manner and evident eagerness to please everyone he came in contact with soon won the affection of the students. He was always delighted when an opportunity presented itself so that he might be of some service to the little charges of the Order. Friendly relations were not only quickly established with the students but with the majority of their parents and relatives who came to visit them at school. The parents always stopped to chat with the doorkeeper and ask him to keep a special watch over their children.

When not occupied at his regular task Brother André made himself useful about the place in many ways. He helped with the washing of the dishes, having become most proficient at the work during the year of his novitiate. At other times he helped with the general cleaning and patched the garments of the members of the faculty or any of the students that appealed to him for aid. At the time there was no regular barber in the vicinity of Cotes Des Neiges and Brother André acted in this capacity. He soon became so expert at hair cutting that he was recognized at the college as the official barber.

His charge for a hair cut was five cents, and his clients included every boy in the school.

A man who was a student at the college during the early days of Brother André's career as "official barber," in describing him said:

"He was always a most lovable, simple soul. His object in life seemed to be to aid the boys in every way and increase their comfort. When one of us kids grew homesick or there was something the matter with us we just naturally seemed to turn to Brother André for sympathy and advice. He certainly did understand boys and in his kindly, gentle way no matter what was annoying us, he would make us forget it. He was really the official barber of the school and let me assure you he was a mighty good one who took great pride in his work. His manner has not changed a bit in all the years that I have known him."

Brother André soon became an important cog in the machinery of the college. Upon generations of students he impressed the relationship between the divine and the human. Although his lack of book learning was well known among the students it in no way affected his influence. His sterling character, pleasing personality and his earnest desire to aid and help them won for Brother

André the genuine respect and affection of
the students. His piety and humility in carrying on the work of God under the most trying
circumstances put the gentle porter in an
exalted position in the eyes of the boys.

His great devotion to Saint Joseph was a
matter of general knowledge about the school.
He rarely missed an opportunity to urge the
students to seek the aid of his patron in their
difficulties. He was ever ready to breathe
his message of faith and devotion into the
ears of the boys who came to him for advice
and their response was really remarkable.
Devotion to Saint Joseph spread rapidly
among the boys. He really became their
patron which was a great tribute to the saintly
old porter.

Soon the parents of the students began to
hear much of Brother André, whose many
kindnesses had endeared him to the boys.
They learned that he delighted in doing
humble works of charity and was always willing and anxious to aid those in distress of
any kind. They heard how after working
hard all day at the various tasks assigned to
him he knelt beside the hard board that
served as his bed until late into the night
praying to Saint Joseph and asking his help.
Further, they heard that this pious brother

denied himself everything that might even remotely suggest luxury and that his menu consisted almost entirely of bread and water.

These stories repeated by the boys excited the interest of their elders and prompted them to seek more information concerning the friendly porter. Those who stopped at the door to chat with him were impressed by his humble simplicity. Many asked to be remembered in his prayers. Such requests seemed to delight him and he always gladly promised to intercede with his patron for them. Some extraordinary favors were granted and it quickly became the custom of those asking Brother André to pray for them to recount to him their spiritual and physical wants. Always when a tale of trouble was thus poured into his ears Brother André would breathe his gospel of faith to the applicant and suggest that a novena be started to Saint Joseph. At the same time he would promise himself to aid in petitioning the head of the Holy Family.

Request after request was granted following the completion of novenas thus started. The result was that the fame of the pious Brother spread like wildfire and resulted in a tremendous increase in the number of persons who journeyed to the college to ask his advice and prayers. He was very happy. His joy was not inspired by the fact that people were coming to him, asking his prayers, but because he felt that now, in some small way he was in a position where he could aid in spreading devotion to his patron. He was untiring in his efforts to comfort the people who came to him and was most anxious to impress upon them the power of prayer.

The work done by Brother André in behalf of his patron attracted considerable attention, as might be expected. The impression prevailed among the superstitious when some really remarkable favors had been granted after prayers by Brother André, that he was endowed with supernatural powers and could cure the sick at will. While, of course, this was not so nor did Brother André wish such an impression to prevail, he soon became the refuge of the sick and afflicted from all parts of Montreal and the surrounding country.

Within a short time the dusty roads leading to Cotes Des Neiges became crowded daily with pilgrims seeking the advice and prayers of the meek old porter and barber. He received those who came in his usual humble, hopeful way. After listening to their troubles he would whisper his message of

CHAPEL WHERE PILGRIMS FLOCKED TO PETITION
SAINT JOSEPH BEFORE THE CRYPT WAS BUILT

faith into their willing ears and urge that the great power of his mighty patron, Saint Joseph, be invoked through earnest prayer. At the same time he would promise to join in the intercessions himself. They came to him from all creeds and from all walks of life imploring his advice and intercession with Saint Joseph to relieve their ills. They went away better for the visit, filled with hope and faith and with a firm conviction that the powerful head of the Holy Family would not turn deaf ears to their prayers and those of Brother André offered in their behalf.

Faith Rewarded

In a short time many remarkable cures were reported. Those which were construed by countless thousands as being of miraculous origin mounted until they became almost daily occurrences. Stories concerning them and the saintly figure of Cote Des Neiges began filtering into Montreal. The events quickly caught the imagination and Brother André was referred to as "The Miracle Man" of Mount Royal. The tales were so widely repeated and circulated that the Canadian press soon realized that the college on the western flank of Mount Royal had become an excellent news source, well worth watch-

ing. Stories printed in the Montreal papers
attracted widespread attention to Brother
André and the work he was doing. It was
not long before everyone in Montreal, Catholic, Protestant and Jew who suffered any
ailment that defied the efforts of medical science sought the aid of Brother André.

The devout old brother was now constantly
beseiged by persons seeking divine intervention for the alleviation of their sufferings.
People ravaged by disease that had defied
the efforts of medical science to combat
were reported cured after talking with Brother
André and joining with him in prayers for
their recovery. The stories of these cures
many of them magnified in the telling, were
widely circulated throughout the Provence
of Quebec and the surrounding country.
The result was that sufferers came in droves
to see the holy missionary of devotion to
Saint Joseph, who had already accomplished
so much good.

The almost continuous procession of pilgrims that called on the aged porter presented
a really serious problem to the college authorities. The very fact that the people came to
see him in such numbers took him from his
regular tasks and others had to be assigned
to his duties. Certain of the influential rel-

atives and friends of the students lodged an
indignant protest with the faculty against
the old doorkeeper being subject to something akin to veneration by persons who considered that he was the possessor of supernatural powers who could cure their ills and
do away with their troubles at will. These
protests or complaints were very strongly
presented and in such a way that they could
not be ignored by the college authorities.

An Attack

The antagonists of the new form of devotion came forward, as persons of their type
have for generations, protesting that their
only object in calling the matter to the attention of the authorities was to save the Catholic Church from being put in a ridiculous
position by the activities of Brother André.
Their tactics were most identical to those employed by the unbelievers who first assailed
the miracles at Lourdes immediately after the
Blessed Virgin had appeared at the Grotto.
They declared that continuance of the pilgrimages to see Brother André was bound
eventually, to put the whole Congregation of
the Holy Cross in a ridiculous position which
would hurt the Church as a whole. They
admitted that they, of course, did not object

to the aged doorkeeper urging greater devotion to Saint Joseph, but at the same time contended that his activities be curbed before the matter had gone too far. Their protests were lodged with the Provincial who was greatly interested in Brother André and regarded him as a saintly character who was a credit to the Order.

While the forces of the opposition were being marshaled and new attacks on Brother André was being launched almost daily, the friends and clients of the modest dispenser of faith had not abandoned him. It was an indignant, shocked group that rallied to the support of the saintly character of Cotes Des Neiges. The most militant of these were persons thoroughly familiar with his life and his works and people who had been granted extraordinary favors after intercession to Saint Joseph at the recommendation of Brother André. They demanded to know what wrong or injury the venerable old brother could work through his intercession and devotion to the powerful head of the Holy Family.

They flung a challenge at the opposition demanding to know from them as Catholics when and where the Catholic Church had ever forbidden the faithful to honor and pray

to Saint Joseph in any way they saw fit. They
could not understand the complaints and
reasoned that the enemies of their beloved
spiritual leader must also be enemies of the
Catholic Church. Among the staunchest de-
fenders of Brother André were many Protestants and Jews of Montreal who knew and
admired him. They made personal visits to
him and offered him every aid. He humbly
explained that he had no enemies and that
if the complaints against him were justified
his superiors would realize it and direct him
to cease receiving the pilgrims.

While the controversy was being bitterly
waged about him Brother André, himself,
gave it scant attention. The only time he
talked of the complaints lodged against him
was when friends came to pledge their support and offer their sympathy. As much as
possible he ignored the controversy as if it
never had been started and continued on,
receiving pilgrims in his usual way, unper-
turbed by the attacks made upon him.

A Crude Shrine

He continued to make his daily pilgrimage
to the rocky, wooded slope of Mount Royal
just across Cote Des Neiges, from the college
where he led his simple self-sacrificing life

in the holy atmosphere. Half way up the rugged hillside in the heart of the dense woods he had fashioned a crude shrine in honor of his patron. He had gathered some jagged stones together and placed them in a pile. He had builded the pile until it was more than five feet high.

Then in the center of it he had placed a little, homely statue of Saint Joseph purchased with the money he had received for his work as barber at the college. To protect his beloved image from the rain, sleet and snow that hurl themselves with such fury against the side of Mount Royal, the godly brother had erected an odd sort of covering or shelter. A flat stone was placed over the statue which looked out from its crude place in the rocks. The shrine reminded one of the simple markers left through the North American Continent by those courageous missionaries whose exploration expeditions marked the march of civilization into the wilds of America. Such a shrine might be found in the wilderness of the Adirondacks or other such places where Christianity's distinguished crusaders had dwelt while they endeavored to rescue the Indians from paganism.

A tiny, twisting path led up the hillside to the shrine. Few knew of it or suspected its existence. It was hidden from the sight of passersby by huge boulders and heavy shrubs. It was there on the bare rocks surrounded by the wild things of nature that the venerable brother retired daily and buried himself in prayer for those who came to him for aid and advice. It was on this steep hillside, lighted by the fading light of the late afternoon sun that Brother André spent much of his time in deep prayer while the controversy concerning him and his work was being bitterly contested. From this lonely retreat he raised his voice to Heaven in behalf of the afflicted, imploring the aid of his patron in relieving their sufferings and asking that numerous blessings be showered down upon them. Often while thus plunged in prayer Brother André remained on the hillside until long after his dinner hour and retired without breaking his fast. However, his tasks at the college were always completed before he thought of going to his cell for the night.

For a considerable time the college authorities pondered over the problem presented to them by the protests concerning the work and activities of Brother André. The first action they took following the complaints of the relatives and friends of the students whose alleged concern for the Church prompted

their action, was to decree that all wishing
to see Brother André must call at other than
school hours. This arrangement proved entirely unsatisfactory and was almost univer-
sally disregarded by those who wished to
consult the old doorkeeper. They continued
to come at the hours most convenient to themselves and crowded the pavilion set aside for
them by the faculty. They came whenever
they were able to make the journey and on
arrival demanded to see Brother André and
receive his advice and blessings. The crippled
and infirm displayed what might have been
construed as contempt for the edict of the
college authorities. Whenever the urge was
strong they went to the college to consult
with and pray with their advisor, regardless of
the hour.

The organized opposition to the spreading
of devotion to Saint Joseph and the endeavors
to curb it did not cease with the announcement of the new regulations by the college
authorities. Instead, the announcement
tended to give the movement, designed to
stamp out the new devotion, added impetus.
All the opposition to the venerable religious,
however, did not come from the relatives of
the students. From within the ranks of his
own Order there was considerable agitation

directed against the continuance of the practice of the doorkeeper in receiving pilgrims who came to him from all walks of life. If such opposition dismayed Brother André he never revealed his feelings but continued with his work as if it had never developed. Just why those in his own household opposed him he did not inquire nor did he give any evidence that he was concerned.

The age old cry was raised that such outward display of devotion as Brother André inspired and advocated, coming from an entirely uneducated religious would lead to great embarrassment and the possible ruination of the whole Congregation of the Holy Cross. In the face of these assaults from without and within his own household the saintly old apostle of faith maintained his usual silence. He ignored the attacks as if they had never been started. He failed utterly to raise his voice to defend himself or his acts and continued to perform his humble tasks as best he could, spending as much time as possible in prayer to his patron. His attitude was certainly irritating to the self-appointed censors of faith and devotion whose attacks had focused attention upon him and at the same time spread knowledge of the work he was carrying out. The fact that he ignored

the assaults and continued his missionary
work as if nothing out of the ordinary had
happened ténded to increase the desire of
the opposition that he be curbed.

With this object in view they sought the
aid of the ecclesiastical authorities. They
made a formal protest to the learned Bishop
Bruchesi of Montreal charging that it was his
duty as a protector of the faith to stop Brother
André before he put the whole church in a
ridiculous and undefendable position. They
demanded a hearing by His Grace. This
was granted and they were given a full opportunity of expressing themselves on the subject. They asserted that their protest was
prompted only by a desire to save the church
from undue criticism and attacks from certain quarters that are always on the alert for
new avenues through which they might
launch their attacks. His Grace listened patiently while they argued against the continuance of Brother André's activities. He
made no comment when they had exhausted
their list of complaints. The very fact that
he took no action, however, was construed by
many as an indication that he gave at least
tentative approval to the work of the aged
porter. He was apparently just watching
developments out at Cotes Des Neiges, and

was not inclined to interfere before he had further information.

Defeated in their efforts to crush the movement to honor Saint Joseph, that was spreading like wildfire throughout Canada, by means of the ecclesiastical authorities, those opposed to Brother André followed the example of the Free Thinkers of France at the time of the appearance of the Blessed Virgin at Lourdes. Their new instrument for stamping out the devotion that was so rapidly gaining favor with the people was the civil authorities.

They lodged a complaint with the Board of Health of the City of Montreal against Brother André and his superiors in the Congregation of the Holy Cross who approved his work. They brazenly charged that the health and lives of the three hundred students were threatened and endangered by following the advice of the old doorkeeper whose sway of influence over them was very great. The language and startling nature of the complaint was such that the municipal authorities actually did start an investigation in 1906. Just how far their inquiry was pushed, or just what line of investigation they followed could not be ascertained. However, this much is known—that it was quickly dropped without action or recommendation.

Brother André, the storm center of this controversy that raged throughout the Province of Quebec never dignified the attacks made upon him by recognizing them. Displaying the passion of one who lives only for others and seeking only more opportunity to spread devotion to his patron, he continued to receive the host of pilgrims that came to him and to breathe his message of faith, hope and love for Saint Joseph. At the same time he continued to distribute his medallions and the holy oil that had been burned before the statue of Saint Joseph and his fame continued to spread. Already it was well established in the realm of the afflicted and they flocked to him by the hundreds pouring into his ears their tales of misery and misfortune. He listened to them attentively and in the simple language of his kind assured them if they had real faith in Saint Joseph, his patron, their ills would be cured and they went away better for their visit.

Cures of a remarkable character were recorded from time to time. The records in most of the important cases together with the authenticating certificates from physicians who had previously treated the persons cured were made and filed away by the priests in charge of the Oratory. At the proper time

they will be presented to an ecclesiastical
tribunal with a view of determining whether
the cures were of supernatural origin or not.
There has been considerable pressure brought
to bear to have these cures officially passed
upon by the Catholic Church in the immediate future.

The attacks on Brother André and the
work he was doing in spreading devotion to
Saint Joseph attracted considerable attention not only among the Catholics but among
the Protestants and Jews of Montreal who
were at all familiar with his accomplishments.
The assaults upon this new dispenser of faith
were deeply resented by these non-Catholics.
Without solicitation of any kind, when they
learned of the edict of the college authorities
in prohibiting Brother André to receive vis-
itors in scholastic hours, they contributed
freely to a fund to erect a chapel where he
might talk with and console the afflicted at
any hour. They offered to do more than that
—they wanted to build him a church and fully
equip it.

These donations coupled with the gifts of
Catholics soon amounted to enough for the
construction of a small frame chapel on the
flank of Mount Royal just above the spot
where for years the kindly old apostle of faith

had knelt on the bare rocks and prayed to Saint Joseph for the intentions of those who came to him. Soon a twisting winding and altogether tortuous path was beaten up the rugged slope by the afflicted who came by the thousands to see him.

The site on the northwestern flank of Mount Royal where the chapel was erected has a most interesting history. The events that led to its purchase by the Congregation of the Holy Cross are worth recording. The Order was created in 1835 through the merger of two religious societies; a group of diocesan missionaries founded by the Rev. Father Antoine-Basile Moreau, Canon of the Cathedral at Mains, France, and a congregation of teaching brothers that came into being in 1820 under the leadership of the Rev. Abbé Dujarie, pastor of Ruille-Sur-Loir and known as the Institute of the Brothers of Saint Joseph. From the time of the merger and indeed, from its creation the organization was pledged in a special way to spread devotion to Saint Joseph. Through the generations that have passed, its mission has been dominated by this idea. In 1847 at the invitation of Bishop Bourget the Congregation of the Holy Cross was introduced into the Montreal diocese. A little band of one

priest and eight teaching brothers came from
the mother house in France and established
their first parochial school at St. Laurent,
just outside of Montreal. This institution
subsequently became the College of St. Laurent, a famous seat of learning in Quebec.

The pioneers brought with them a great
devotion to the foster-father of Jesus. This
was highly pleasing to the learned Bishop
Bourget who was ever zealous for means to
spread devotion to Saint Joseph. In 1855,
in writing the decrees of the second plenary
provincial of Quebec he said in part:

St. Joseph, then, must have a church which will
in a certain sense supply the service of all the
others, and in which he may receive every day the
public honors due to his eminent virtues. . . .
We wish to consecrate whatever is left to us of
strength and life in the task of having him honored
in such a church and of making that church a
place of pilgrimage whither the faithful will come
to visit him even as they now visit his glorious
spouse in the church of Bonsecours.

Little did this saintly character in Canadian
Church history realize to what extent his
prophecy would be fulfilled within a couple
of generations. Nor could he foresee that
a great basilica would soon tower over the

lofty top of Mount Royal where hosts of the faithful would daily gather to raise their voices in pleas to their mighty patron.

From the beginning of Brother André's assignment at Cotes Des Neiges the college authorities were anxious to acquire the land across the road from the institution where the shrine now stands. During the early seventies Montreal contained numerous clubs and other places of amusement that were not especially designed to elevate the mind or body. Several of these were located in the immediate vicinity of the college and the faculty feared that the desirable site across the road might be utilized to bring the growing menace to the youth of the community right to their door. To forestall such action repeated attempts were made to secure the property without success. The resources of the community were limited and the price asked by the owner seemed exorbitant. Even when the property changed hands and was acquired by a French-Canadian the asking price was so high that for several years the project was abandoned, for the time.

One day while the late Brother Alderic was walking through the property with his superior the Rev. Father Geoffrion, he stopped on the hillside and buried a tiny medal of Saint

INTERIOR OF THE CRYPT OF SAINT JOSEPH'S ORATORY

Joseph.   Brother André and others of the
Order who made it a practice to stroll through
the place also buried little medals in the
ground and the whole Congregation seemed
to renew its prayers that the property would
be acquired.   Finally in 1896 the purchase
was effected.   When it was finally bought the
faculty was confronted with the problem of
just what to do with the eighteen acres, most
of which was covered with heavy timber.
It was decided that the lower part should be
cultivated and that the rugged hillside be
left in its natural state as a playground and
recreation center for the faculty and students.

For several years previous to the starting
of the little frame chapel in 1904, Brother
André had made repeated attempts to impress upon the authorities the desirability of
such a structure on the hillside.   All such
requests had been flatly denied partly because of the expense involved and partly
because by the erection of the chapel, the
faculty would be officially recognizing and
approving of a movement that thus far had
simply been tolerated.

The First Chapel

It happened that Brother André was
stricken with one of his frequent spells of ill-

ness at the same time that his superior, Father Lecavalier was a patient in the infirmary of the college. The two religious were, of course, much in each other's company during their period of convalescence and naturally talked of many of the things most dear to their hearts. The favorite subject and thought of Brother André was Saint Joseph and he talked much of the patron. Father Lecavalier was deeply impressed by the simple, childlike devotion of the brother and listened long to his earnest pleas for the authority to construct a chapel where the Protector of the Holy Family might be honored in a special way.

Father Lecavalier finally gave him permission to use the college carpenter for the erection of the chapel and at the same time authorized the spending of the two hundred dollars he had saved from his earnings as a barber for the boys in the institution. As soon as this became known it was apparent that Brother André was not the only one who had dreamed of the erection of a sanctuary to the patron on the hillside. As heretofore mentioned hundreds of those who had prayed with him in the little college chapel formed themselves into an unofficial committee and contributed freely to the cost of the building.

The two hundred dollars of the modest porter did not go far toward the building of the structure. However, to the faithful workmen engaged on the work these hard earned dollars seemed an inexhaustible fund. After being paid each Saturday they would eagerly inquire:

"Shall we return to work on Monday, Brother?"

His frequent reply was that he did not know what to do and then they would declare their loyalty to him and their faith in the mighty patron to provide him with the funds to pay them. In all the time they worked on the structure only one week passed when the contributions were not a little more than sufficient to take care of the payroll. When the workers did not get their pay promptly they were not disappointed and came to work on the following Monday as if nothing out of the ordinary had happened. During that week the donations for the chapel flowed in and at its conclusion they were paid for two weeks.

It is worth noting here that one of the first cures recorded at the spot, occurred just after the work preparatory to the building of the first chapel was started. A young man named Calixte Richard, visited his uncle who was a brother in the College of Notre

Dame about the time Brother André was starting the work for his chapel. He suffered from a severe case of chronic dyspepsia and was in a greatly weakened condition. His haggard face attracted the attention of Brother André who was himself in great difficulty because of lack of sufficient funds. The modest porter wanted to construct a wagon road to the top of the hill where his chapel was to be built. To save money he decided he would do the job himself with the aid of one workman. At noontime on the first day the laborer he employed quit. Then he realized he needed at least one skilled in sapping and mining to make any progress with the work.

It was just at that time that Calixte Richard appeared. The fact that he was a skilled quarry hand was conveyed to Brother André by the uncle of the youth. Ignoring the apparent weakness of the youth the brother asked if he would go to work on the road. The sick man declared that he would like nothing better but added that his physical condition had been such for the past three and a half years that he had not been able to do any work.

The brother was disappointed but told the youth that even if he could not work he could look over the job and perhaps offer some suggestions. They walked toward the foot of the hill discussing the difficulties of the task. Suddenly Brother André inquired:

"If Saint Joseph would cure you would you work for him?"

Failing to grasp the meaning of the question Richard hesitated in his reply, finally saying, "I am not able."

Again Brother André repeated the question and this time promptly received an affirmative reply.

"Very well, then," said Brother André, "get to work."

The man who had not labored in over three years again took up the hard work of a quarry worker with no apparent effort. He did not miss a day for five months until the chapel was dedicated.

The chapel was dedicated by the vicar-general of the diocese of Montreal, the late Mgr. Racicot in November, 1904. It was a simple little place, in a clearing among the rugged rocks high up on the hill. It was not much more than a square shed being fifteen feet wide and eighteen feet deep. The installation of windows would have added to the expense, therefore they were abandoned. The only light filtered in through skylights arranged in primitive fashion in the roof. The building was without regular doors but the side opening on the face of the mountain could be thrown back permitting the congregation to hear mass while they stood in the open. Several rows of benches were placed facing this opening.

The altar was simple, being made of the same material that went into the rest of the structure. The only decoration on the day of dedication was a large statue of Saint Joseph that was carried in the procession. This was placed over the altar where it still remains. The first mass was offered up by the Rev. Father Geoffrion, C.S.C., and the congregation was made up of the priests and brothers of the Order, the students of the college and groups of the faithful who were interested in and had helped Brother André with the project.

Immediately after the opening of the chapel it had to be closed for the winter because, of course, no heating facilities had been installed. It was from this humble beginning that the Oratory of Saint Joseph, now the greatest place of pilgrimage in the world arose. The progress of this remarkable shrine, the fruit of the sublime faith of a saintly old man, is recorded elsewhere in this narrative.

II

𝕮𝖍𝖊 𝕺𝖗𝖆𝖙𝖔𝖗𝖞

FROM the time of the construction of the
first humble wooden chapel, heretofore described in 1904, St. Joseph's Oratory has
advanced with amazing rapidity until now the
plans for the greatest Basilica on the North
American continent have been drawn and the
actual work started.

When the weather permitted in the Spring
of 1905, the ardent pilgrims again flocked to
ask the aid of the pious, uneducated Brother
André. His fame and the fame of his patron
had indeed spread as indicated by the constant stream of sufferers who trudged up the
rocky path to the tiny chapel in the woods.
He spent all his leisure time there, which
means that he was there constantly when his
duties as doorkeeper at the college did not
detain him. He was not relieved of his assignment at the door of the education institution
until 1909. Then the demands made upon

his time were so great that his superiors could not help but recognize the necessity of allowing the pilgrims to see him whenever they wished.

The first of the organized pilgrimages that are now an inspiring feature of the Oratory was organized in 1905. It was a pilgrimage of Montreal men and women who were familiar with the work being carried on by Brother André and of the results he accomplished. The leader of this movement was a layman who had long been interested in the pious porter. The second pilgrimage was under the leadership of Abbé Perrault, of the parish of Cotes Des Neiges which was very large. While the Mass was being celebrated for this gathering, a storm of marked intensity broke and the faithful were forced to scurry for shelter. The little chapel could protect but a small part of the crowd and the urgent need of greater facilities for the pilgrims was impressed on all. The crowds continued to storm this rocky cliff where faith reigned supreme during the Summer and plans for expansion were formulated. That the space for the accommodation of the faithful was inadequate was frankly admitted and the authorities at the Oratory with their limited means strove to improve conditions.

The Rev. Father Dion, Provincial of the
Congregation of the Holy Cross, who had
made his headquarters at St. Laurent, was
carefully watching and studying the work
being done by Brother André out at Cote
Des Neiges. That he was impressed by it
was evidenced by the fact that in 1906 he
transferred his office to the College of Our
Lady where he might make better observations of the happenings. His great concern in the beginning was for the future of the
Congregation but when he became familiar
from first-hand knowledge of the work of
Brother André he became an ardent supporter
of the old religious. This sombre, thoughtful
student became a real builder of the Oratory
as soon as he studied and realized the possibil-
ities of the shrine that was growing under his
very eyes. He was a man of vision and tact,
just the type needed for the situation. Although among his outstanding characteristics were his piety and devotion to the Church
and his Order, he was not one who might be
swayed by emotion. He was the ideal type for
the work that confronted him and he did it
well.

In his preliminary survey of the situation
Father Dion directed that the crutches and
other implements of misfortune that had

been left in the little chapel by privileged clients of Saint Joseph be removed. Brother André entered a strong but respectful protest with his superior regarding this order. The Provincial listened patiently and then deciding that his judgment had erred, he revoked the order and the ex-votos were restored to their former places. This was really the first inquiry of a religious character into the work being carried on by Brother André and the revoking of the decree certainly was a victory for him.

The pilgrims in large numbers protested to Brother André concerning the smallness of the place of worship and urged that it be enlarged. At their suggestion he applied to the Archbishop of Montreal for permission to broaden the work and to keep the chapel open constantly for the faithful. That dignitary, however, after hearing the facts decided that the time was not ripe for a definite decision from him on the matter and he declined to authorize the enlargement of the chapel. He had already listened to many conflicting reports concerning Brother André and his work and could not just then make up his mind as to the proper course to pursue. Thus matters rested until 1907.

Then a committee of distinguished laymen

called on the Provincial with a demand that the chapel be enlarged to accommodate the numerous clients of Saint Joseph who were anxious to see the work progress. Father Dion, with great sympathy listened to their pleas and promised to take them up with the diocesan authorities. He did take the matter up immediately and subsequently in reporting the result of his application wrote:

"A few days ago I submitted to His Grace the Archbishop the project which your piety towards Saint Joseph has suggested to you. Here is what His Grace said to me in reply: 'Before permitting the erection of a public sanctuary, I desire to see its plan and to know the approximate cost. Moreover, I insist that the sum necessary for the construction of this church be well guaranteed beforehand.'

"The Archbishop added that, because of the many diocesan works which have to be supported by the offerings of the faithful, he could allow no collection in the diocese for the church in question. Besides, the ownership of the church would reside in the College of Our Lady, which should charge itself with the maintenance of worship therein."

Thus His Grace clarified the situation. He no longer objected to the construction of a great shrine church to Saint Joseph on Mount Royal. His only concern was the financial problem. He did not want the shrine church started, and then have the burden of finishing it thrust on his already overburdened diocese, and finally he wanted the title of the structure vested in religious and not in laymen. Work was delayed for many reasons. The Congregation did not feel that it could assume any additional financial obligations and the laymen who were interested did not have sufficient funds to pledge that would guarantee the building costs without making appeals to the diocese which were forbidden by the decree of His Grace.

The Shrine Grows

The same conditions prevailed during the years of 1907–1909. During the winter seasons the chapel was closed, the cold being unbearable. Each spring, however, the pilgrims flocked back to the shrine in ever-increasing numbers. The situation was unsatisfactory to all concerned. Often hundreds of worshipers were exposed to the disagreeable variations of the Montreal climate in the spring and fall. Numerous meetings were held with a view of bettering conditions. It was finally decided to erect a simple shelter. The cost decided the type it must be and during July, 1909, an ordinary shed supported

by heavy posts was erected on the mountain-
side near the chapel. The shed was one hundred feet long and forty feet wide.

During the summer when the tourists from
the United States flocked into Montreal the
donations increased greatly and the money
was available for the boarding up of the sides
of the shed. This formed a nave for the original chapel and arrangements for heating
the entire structure were completed. Thus
for the first time the little shrine church was
made available for worship all year round
regardless of the weather.

The year of 1909 was a really important one
in the life of Brother André and the Oratory.
The pavilion, described elsewhere in this
book, containing a restaurant and office for
Brother André was completed. At the same
time the humble porter and barber of the
college was relieved of his former duties and
assigned as caretaker of the Oratory so that
he was available at all times for interviews
with the pilgrims. From that time on the
shrine church expanded rapidly.

During the winter the host of pilgrims that
came to the sanctuary was so great that
the religious in charge quickly realized that
they would be utterly unable to accommodate
the summer throngs. More of the shed was

enclosed and a real effort was made to convert the simple shed into a church and vest it with the dignity befitting such a place. During the following three years further additions had to be made to the original chapel and shed to accommodate the hundreds of clients of Saint Joseph who came to consult the humble brother. When the latest addition was blessed by Archbishop Bruchesi himself late in November, His Grace for the first time indicated that the religious authorities had in any way recognized the extraordinary events on Mount Royal when he said:

"I behold here a movement of piety which greatly consoles me. This Oratory may justly be compared with the mustard seed which, so small in itself, nevertheless grows till it becomes a great tree.

"In the beginning a simple and pious hand placed here a statue; then daily prayer was offered here; soon a little chapel was built. St. Joseph's clients becoming more numerous, the chapel had to be enlarged, and more than once. It is this latest addition which I have come to bless today.

"This work, however, is only in its infancy. I foresee in the future that cannot be far distant, a church, a basilica worthy of St. Joseph, rising here on Mount Royal and facing the most magnificent of horizons.

"Shall I say that miracles are wrought here? Were I to deny that such is the case, I would be contradicted by all these instruments and ex-votos, witnesses of all species of suffering. I have no need of an investigation to declare extraordinary events are taking place here. There are being wrought greater prodigies than bodily cures—about which cures I admit that one may be easily deceived; but far greater than the physical are the spiritual cures effected here. Sinners have come here, and after praying have gone to confession and returned to their homes purified.

"I strongly advise you to come here frequently to pray. Come, yourselves, and bring your relatives, your friends and acquaintances."

While these utterances of the Archbishop were construed by many as the first official approval of the Catholic Church on the work of Brother André, it is known that in 1910, His Grace appointed a canonical commission of inquiry to investigate the information reaching him concerning the events at the Oratory. The members of this commission were three distinguished ecclesiastics whose findings would be indisputable; Rev. Joseph Lalande, S. J., rector of St. Mary's College; the late Canon Savaria, pastor at Lachine and Abbé Philippe Perrier, of the parish of Saint-

Enfant Jesus. At the time Abbé Perrier was general visitor of the schools of Montreal.

An exhaustive investigation was made and a complete report was delivered to His Grace in 1911. This report with the approval of the Archbishop was made public. The question of the authenticity of the cures reported to have taken place at the Oratory was not established by it nor were they pronounced as miracles. It was declared, however, that the devotion to St. Joseph was practiced as the Oratory was in entire conformity with the teachings and dignity of the church. In conclusion a great tribute was paid to the inspiring faith and humble piety of Brother André and the faithful were granted permission and even urged to intercede with the carpenter of Nazareth, at the Oratory.

In the spring of 1915 when Canada was staggering under the frightful blow of her losses during the conflict in Europe, the preparations for the construction of a great basilica progressed so that work on a vast crypt designed to be part of the mighty shrine was started. This crypt is now completed and will serve the pilgrims until the great basilica is constucted.

In conclusion let it be stated that the Oratory is being erected entirely from voluntary

A MIGHTY PILGRIMAGE PAYS TRIBUTE TO THE POWERFUL PATRON OF THE ORATORY

contributions from persons who come to it as pilgrims. Its completion will involve more than two millions of dollars, most of which has been pledged. The only regular sources of revenue outside the collections are the dues paid in the Confraternity of Saint Joseph, which has about 15,000 members and from the *Annals* which records the progress of the shrine. The *Annals* has a monthly circulation of approximately 35,000.

Some idea of the fame of the Oratory may be gleaned from the fact that Brother André receives about 40,000 letters and communications annually from all parts of the world. Four secretaries are constantly engaged in handling the correspondence. Most of the letters are read to the aged brother and he indicates what his reply should be. That he will live to see the completion of the great shrine is the hope of the thousands who have found divine consolation in the citadel of faith he made possible.

III

The Pilgrims

CONSIDERING the short span of years during which pilgrims have found divine attraction at the sanctuary of Saint Joseph's Oratory, the development of the Shrine as the greatest place of pilgrimage in Christendom seems almost incredible. However, the fact remains that within one generation, practically without publicity, the Oratory has risen from obscurity as a place of pilgrimage until it now surpasses Lourdes and other famed shrines of the Continent in the numbers annually attracted to its altars.

There are many reasons for the astounding growth of the Oratory as a haven for the afflicted of the World. The first and most important reason, is the firm conviction among the faithful that Saint Joseph has especially chosen this bleak hillside for manifestations of his miracle working power.

From the beginning of time men have worshiped the visibly wonderful, the witnessing of the physical impossibility before their eyes. They have ever been ready to prostrate themselves before the wonder-worker even though he be an evil genius. But at the beautiful Oratory on the flank of Mount Royal, they have witnessed the miracle working power of the head of the Holy Family and not the deceptive operations of some worldly fakir. They have seen their own people, their relatives and neighbors drag their disease-ridden bodies to the Oratory with death hovering in the not distant future and prostrate themselves before the sanctuary and beg the intercession of the patron to relieve their ills. They have seen these faithful restored to health when medicine had abandoned them as lost. They are the living, walking, ever-present proof and reminders of the miraculous powers of the patron.

The fact that the Oratory is situated in the commercial metropolis of Canada, a country for centuries under the patronage of Saint Joseph, of course, has contributed greatly to the growth of the shrine. The setting for a great center of devotion to Saint Joseph is, indeed, ideal. Approximately ninety per cent of the population of Montreal is Catholic. The first white men to push their way through the wilderness and reach the famous island city were Catholic priests. By grant the French kings gave them the land. At one time the various missionary orders of Catholic priests owned the entire City of Montreal. The people are intensely Catholic. To them their faith is more than life itself. The inhabitants of the surrounding country are French-Canadians. They are almost entirely Catholic. Thus it can be readily seen that this great Oratory of Saint Joseph is located at or near the center of Catholic population on the North American continent.

While the great Catholic population in the immediate vicinity of the shrine contributes largely to the throngs that daily prostrate themselves before the sanctuary and invoke the powers of Saint Joseph, during the summer months pilgrims from the United States and Europe seem to predominate. Considering the utter lack of newspaper publicity concerning the remarkable happenings at the Oratory during the last decade and the general lack of knowledge among Catholics in the United States of its existence, the large number of Americans and other foreigners present during the Summer exercises causes much wonder among observers.

The Oratory is rarely without its clients no

matter what the hour. Pilgrims arriving from afar, many of them after having undergone severe hardships and inconveniences, can remain but a short while. They come to kneel before the shrine in the Crypt that clings to the rocky cliffs just below where the great Basilica will soon tower. Many of this type of the faithful hasten to the Oratory as soon as they reach Montreal, regardless of the hour.

The result is that from sunrise until late into the night, the quaint horse drawn vehicles which largely supply the transportation needs of the tourists in Montreal can be seen laboriously making their way up the steep, sweeping road to the Oratory. Once arriving in this citadel of faith, the pilgrim is immediately impressed by visible signs of the extraordinary powers and goodness of the Protector of the Holy Family. Piles of crutches and other devices of the afflicted that have been cast aside when the prayers of their owners have been answered, meet the eye on every side. The pilgrim has reached his goal and is swept on toward the sanctuary by the flood tide of faith that whirls about him.

To convey to the reader a true picture of this haven of faith and devotion the writer determined to simply record his observations of what takes place on an ordinary day when there are no large pilgrimages. In this way a pen picture of the famed shrine can best be presented.

A Day at the Shrine

As the first rays of the sun penetrate the slowly rising mist and tint the Eastern sky a dull red hue, the priests and brothers of the Congregation of the Holy Cross, in charge of the Oratory have already completed preparations for the long series of High Masses that greet each dawn. In a bare, simple chapel, hidden away in the belfry Mass has already been started. There is no room for a congregation in this tiny place of worship, with its severe lines and marked simplicity. Only a few of the hard working brothers of the Order are present. Two of them are serving the priest and others are deep in prayer. Theirs are lives of great sacrifices and prayer and they glory in it.

Off to one side, kneeling on the hard bare floor, is the pious Brother André. His head is bowed in prayer. He is asking the blessing of his patron on those pilgrims who have recommended themselves to him. The silence in the little chapel, except for the voices of the priest and his servers, is in itself impressive. The very air seems to be charged with faith and a certain holiness as these men of God who have turned their backs on all worldly pleasures and achievements that they might better serve their Maker, begin their day with prayer and devotion.

Outside, far down the windswept mountain-side in the light of the early dawn the first of the long, thin line of pilgrims can be seen making their way over the dusty roads to the Oratory. Others having reached the entrance are bowing as they pass the towering statue of the patron near the main gate. They are making their way painfully, haltingly, in the uncertain light toward the hundred steps that intersect the sweeping driveways up the steep embankment. On the bare wooden steps, still coated with the early morning frost here and there can be seen ardent pilgrims approaching the shrine on bended knees. They pause on each step offering a fervent prayer for the granting of their particular intention.

The vast majority of the pilgrims start their morning petitions before the majestic statue of the patron directly inside the main gate. Many devoutly kneel on the gravel walk before the image. There in the open they commence repeating their prayers which they continue to recite as they walk with bowed heads toward the great flight of steps leading to the heights.

Mingled with the pilgrims can be seen the black robed priests and brothers of the Congregation of the Holy Cross. In their sober cassocks, great black caped coats and quaint hats the religious give a picturesque touch to the scene. As they proceed toward the Crypt, here and there one of them is seen to stop and exchange greetings with the early pilgrims or perhaps to breathe a word of encouragement to some sufferer who laboriously is attempting to reach the church before Mass is started.

As the early morning light floods over the wooded peak of Mount Royal revealing the stern, plain lines of the Crypt, the massive dull gray edifice arrests the attention. Already the great solid oak doors are swinging to and fro as breathless pilgrims reach the heights and enter the shrine church. From within the catacombic structure there filters in childish tones the Latin responses of the altar boys, familiar to Catholics the world over. The deep voice of the priest echoes and re-echoes through the low building. When the voices from the altar are not audible, a strange silence fills the place. The faithful with their heads bowed in prayer seem intense as they voice their pleas for special graces to the mighty protector of the Holy Family.

These clients of Saint Joseph form a polyglot throng. They have journeyed from distant parts of Canada, the United States and Europe, that they might be able to intercede with Saint Joseph here, at the spot where he has already so well evidenced his power and goodness. Among the suppliants are many old men and women, their aged bodies racked by sufferings they hope will be alleviated through divine intervention. Some are supported by youthful relatives and friends. Others, not so fortunate in securing aid, although needing it badly, have come alone and unattended. In this haven of suffering and hope they get scant attention from the more fortunate.

However, the rhythmical tap of crutches on the hard gravel walk and pavement is not heard wholly because of the approach of the aged pilgrims. Indeed, it seems as if the vast majority of the supplicants seeking divine aid have been stricken in youth. As they trudge painfully, sorrowfully, yet filled with hope, up the rugged mountain side, a chain of misery, they present a pitiful sight. Some of them are really too weak to walk. They could not under ordinary circumstances but on this mission they seem buoyed up by faith, a beautiful inspiring faith in Saint Joseph and a firm conviction that the mighty patron will cure all their ills and restore their broken health. How often this faith is rewarded!

The bulk of the crowds is made up of French Canadians. They are a devout Catholic people who breathe their prayers in their native French. Theirs is a great faith that has survived centuries of persecution. To many of them devotion to Saint Joseph, the patron, is like a great passion that consumes their whole beings. They plead for divine help with an intensity entirely foreign to the Anglo-Saxon. The flame of their wonderful faith which could not be extinguished by any form of persecution is more than faith as Americans know it, it is life itself.

Here and there in the pious crowd can be seen a light haired Englishman, an entirely different type, calmly repeating the prayers of the rosary as he holds the beads in his hands. His faith perhaps is as great as that of his co-religionists of French extraction, but by breeding and temperament he is unexpressive. Scattered through the congregation are many dark-faced Latins, mostly Italians. They are people of great and absolute faith who ignore their surroundings as they petition the powerful patron of the shrine to hear their prayers and grant them the graces they seek. There are also many Americans present, more calm and less conspicuous but just as sincere and with as great faith as any of the others.

Surely, at the Oratory poverty rubs elbows with riches. The costly limousines of the wealthy supplicants coming from afar often abruptly halt on the steep incline leading to the shrine to allow some humble pilgrim in the quaint, simple attire of old Quebec to pass on his way to church. The petitioners represent all classes and creeds. They come from every station in life, the sturdy and the afflicted all with the same devotion and confidence in the mercy of the patron in granting the much sought graces.

Inside the Crypt on the main altar under the towering statue of Saint Joseph, the first of the High Masses has started. Several hundred persons are already in the church at this early hour. The majority of them have traveled from distant parts of the city without breaking their fast. They will receive Holy Communion. The celebrant of the Mass is not called upon to distribute the Eucharist. That would delay the starting of the next Mass and other priests waiting their turn to say Mass take charge of this important function. The altar rail is thronged quickly and many unable to reach it devoutly kneel in the aisles as the priests pass. The scene is impressive, the devotion of the people seems to be communicated to observers. They are witnessing the practice of the faith that has survived ages of bitter persecution.

Soon after the first of the pilgrims reached the shrine a slim, frail old man with a great black cloak wrapped about him emerged from the rectory at the right. Far below the average height, this man whose sparse gray hair is brushed back from a high forehead peered through the uncertain light of the breaking day in the direction from whence the pilgrims were coming. His eyes blaze with the light of faith and love. A smile of intense satisfaction plays on his deep lined face. His head is slightly pitched forward as he gazes at those early arrivals. The figure described is that of the venerable Brother André whose mighty faith in the Protector of the Holy Family is responsible for the erection of the Oratory.

This shrunken, pious old man whose system has been racked by dyspepsia since he was ten years old is an early riser. Summer and winter he attends the five o'clock Mass at the little private chapel in the tower of the Crypt. Immediately thereafter he returns to the rectory for a light breakfast—Brother André told the writer that he rarely eats anything except crackers and milk and sometimes a small portion of meat—and then starts in on his correspondence. The communications are read to him and he quickly indicates what he thinks the reply should be. He insists that each letter be read and always replies to them no matter how trivial. Because of his failing eyesight and shaking hand most of the replies are stamped with his signature. A few of them he signs with great effort, generally kneeling on the floor in front of the desk while he affixes in a scrawling hand his signature.

The correspondence keeps Brother André busy until about nine-thirty. Then he prepares to go out to see those who flock to visit him. Until about two years ago (1922) he so arranged his affairs that he was available to talk with the faithful at almost any hour. However, his failing health made continuance of this practice impossible. His physicians decreed that he could not spend more than two hours a day talking with, advising and consoling the pilgrims. In speaking of this edict of the doctors Brother André said:

"The doctors have told me that I should not spend more than two hours a day talking with the people, one hour in the morning and one in the afternoon. How can I do as they say when so many come to see me? Many of them are very poor and they cannot come often. I must see them when they can come here.

"Every day I go out to them about ten o'clock and talk with them until after noon time. Then I come back to the rectory to rest for a while and eat, a little, not much. At two o'clock I go back and sometimes I stay until as late as six or seven o'clock. I must do this, so many come who wish to recommend themselves to Saint Joseph."

Tales of Trouble

The place where Brother André receives and talks to the pilgrims is scarcely more than a shed. It is a rickety structure that seems to cling to the side of the cliff by the aid of some mysterious power. It is badly in need of repair and especially a coat of paint. The sliding glass windows rattle as the wind sweeps up the mountainside and the floor continuously groans a protest under the weight of the clients of Saint Joseph who crowd it daily seeking audiences with the holy Brother.

Just inside the door an old French woman has a stand where she dispenses candy, ice cream and soft drinks to the weary throng tired from their long struggle up the mountainside. Plain wooden benches that creak complainingly when occupied are scattered about the front part of the shed. The whole place is about fifteen feet long and about as wide.

As Brother André enters, the crowd is silent. He looks lovingly at the people and smiles a greeting. He makes his way to a tiny almost bare room on the right where at times he talks with the people. "There is Brother André," the crowd murmurs in unison. At the same time the people push forward eager to be among the first to talk with the saintly man.

As he disappears through the door a murmur runs through the throng. He is gone from sight only a moment. He has discarded his cloak when he reappears and is clad in a well worn cassock. Again the shed is silent and all eyes are focused on the little old man.

Quickly the great apostle of devotion to Saint Joseph reaches his place behind a sort of a counter. For a moment he turns his gaze inquiringly over the people and then as a woman approaches and starts to talk to him excitedly and rapidly in her native French he bows his head and listens attentively to what she is telling him. Without lifting his head Brother André pours forth his doctrine of faith into the willing ears of the woman. He speaks rapidly in French and the woman listens intently to all he has to say. The interview is brief and after a hurried word of thanks she walks away, fortified with a faith and hope she never knew before. To most of the pilgrims Brother André recommends that they say a novena to Saint Joseph and urges that they use some of the sacred oil of the patron which is obtainable at the Oratory. He promises to join in the prayers for the graces sought.

As the woman described above left Brother André, off to one side on a bench a frail boy was observed facing in the direction of the old man. His mother sat with him, her arms about his shoulders. She leans over and whispers something into his ear. His handsome face is immediately lighted up with a smile. The blank frigid stare of his unseeing eyes is pitiful. Brother André beckons for the mother to approach. She seems startled by the summons but quickly recovers herself and with her arm still about the little sufferer she walks toward the great apostle of faith. She speaks rapidly in French and Brother André attentively listens to her recital of the history of the case.

The child was born blind. The resources of the poor family have been almost exhausted

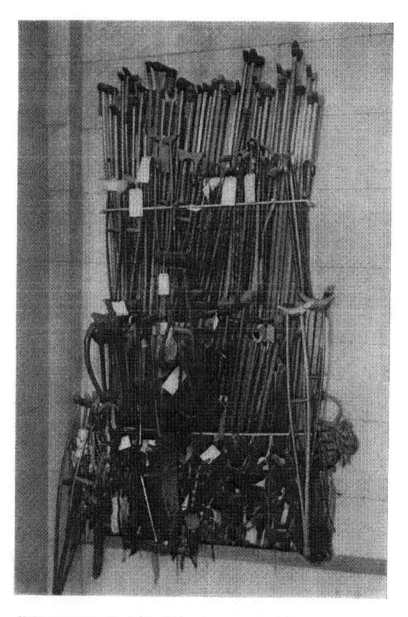

IMPLEMENTS OF THE AFFLICTED DISCARDED BY JOYOUS
OWNERS WHOSE PRAYERS WERE ANSWERED

in futile efforts to aid him. Medical science
has long since abandoned the case. The
learned surgeons had announced there was
nothing they could do for the boy. The
mother refuses to believe them; she explains
she feels that her son is to be given his sight.
She has come to ask the aid of Saint Joseph.
Her faith is inspiring. It is absolute.

Brother André is plainly touched by the
tale of the mother. Her faith in the patron
especially appeals to him. He looks at the
boy for a moment and passes his hand before
the unseeing eyes. Slowly he turns and
speaks to the mother. Her expression changes
and a smile appears on the face that looked
as if it had had little to smile about in life.
She joyously whispered to her son again and
he in turn clapped his chubby hands together.
What the pious old man said, of course, is not
known. His words, however, surely filled
the couple with hope and confidence. They
turned away, the boy's face beaming and little
tears of joy stole down the cheek of the mother
as she led her afflicted son down the three well
worn wooden steps from the shed and walked
toward the Crypt. Within a few minutes the
pair were prostrated before the huge statue in
the shrine church pouring forth their petitions
to the mighty patron.

Brother André looked longingly after the departing pair. Then he turned abruptly and walked into the little private office where he often receives clients. The door had scarcely closed when a young woman in her early twenties stepped toward it. Her frame was so wasted by disease that she seemed a mere human shred. Her left leg was badly twisted and hung helpless. She walked only with the aid of a heavy cane almost dragging the crippled limb after her. She was indeed an object of pity. Timidly she knocked at the door and it was opened by Brother André. She enters and the murmur of voices is heard in the room. Soon she reappears, accompanied by the holy man who is still talking rapidly to her in a low tone. They halt and converse earnestly. Then he tells her to discard her cane and walk.

The woman is afraid and insists she cannot do as she is commanded. Brother André convinces her that she does not need the cane and she carefully puts it down on a bench and haltingly takes a few steps toward the center of the room. As she realizes she can move without the aid of the cane her eyes blaze with joy. Her face is turned heavenward as if her very soul is raised in thanksgiving. The fact that the eyes of a goodly crowd are focused on her means nothing. She seems unconscious of all earthly things. And then in a second as if the spell had been broken she crumpled to the floor a helpless wreck. She quickly struggled to her feet without aid and sat down to recover herself. Then she walked a few more steps without the aid of a cane.

Brother André walked over to her and spoke. He told her to leave her cane at the Crypt and in convincing tones said to her that she would have no further use for it. The people crowded about her as she left eagerly inquiring if she felt she was cured. Several prompted by curiosity sought to halt her on her way to the church and question her concerning the length of her illness and the cause. That afternoon after Benediction in the Crypt the youthful sufferer left the heavy cane, a symbol of her affliction in the church and departed with scarcely any trace of her great affliction.

In the vast multitude who seek Brother André the great majority have been drawn to the shrine by faith. They are believers who are sufferers from every form of disease and affliction. When these observations were recorded, however, Montreal was filled with tourists and many of these are attracted to the scene entirely by curiosity. Some of the latter unable to veil their intolerance, in hushed tones jested with companions at the ardent faith of the pilgrims. The sneers of the unbelievers seemed so out of place and so ill becoming, however, in such surroundings that for the most part they passed unnoticed. They offer no explanation for the remarkable cures that have taken place at the Oratory, except to say that science could account for them. Just how, they were unable to say in view of the authenticating affidavits of learned physicians and surgeons not of the Catholic faith.

In the patient crowd that sat on the hard benches for a moment with Brother André, was a little woman, aged much beyond her years. Although her clothes were old and patched and her hat ancient there seemed to be a certain nobility in her poverty. On the bench beside her was a tiny girl with a great sore on her face that distorted her mouth. The child was wasted beyond description. It seemed as if her eyes alone were still alive and that they burned with a great love and faith for the patron of the Oratory. The terrible disease that appeared to be devouring the child had respected her beautiful long black hair that hung like a royal mantle down over her tattered garments.

The gentle, kindly way the ever humble and

sympathetic Brother André received these
poverty stricken pilgrims was a revelation.
When they left him the tears no longer welled
in the eyes of the child. She and her mother
were calm and there was a look of faith and
hope in the eyes of the mother that had never
been there before. That afternoon I saw the
pair at Benediction in the Crypt. They were
praying devoutly to Saint Joseph.

The crowds continue to invade the little
shed where Brother André is still holding audiences with the faithful who have come to recommend themselves to Saint Joseph. The
lines of misery and suffering that pass before
the holy servant of God seem unending.
Every type and condition of disease is represented and the afflicted all by their faces and
attitude indicate their absolute faith in the
cures they pray and hope for.

A consumptive youth with a hacking cough
accompanied by an aged mother earnestly
listened to what Brother André had to say
after they briefly related the history of the
case. They went away filled with hope and
confidence, their faces beaming happiness to
pray before the shrine. Next came a middle
aged man whose hearing was defective. He
declared that the doctors had failed to aid
him and that the progress of the disease was

robbing him of his means of livelihood. To him as to the others Brother André breathed words of hope and faith.

Always he urges prayer to Saint Joseph and the application of the holy oil of the patron which is obtainable at the Oratory. Absolute faith in the power and goodness of the Protector of the Holy Family is essential to all cures he declares. His language is simple and direct. There can be no mistaking his advice. They go away better for the visit, to pray with a faith they have never known before and with the utmost confidence that their prayers will be answered.

A powerfully built man, evidently a French-Canadian farmer, was seen to walk over to Brother André. His son, a frail lad of about eight with a great vacant stare in his eyes was at his side. That the boy's mentality was very low was apparent. He clutched at persons who were near him. He held on to the dress of a woman. She spoke kindly to him and he snatched her hat. His father intent on talking to Brother André turned to see what had happened. The child refused to give up the hat until forced to.

The parent explained to the woman that his son had never shown signs of advancing mentally since he was an infant. The scant resources of the family had been almost exhausted in futile consultations and remedies. He had the sympathy of the onlookers. He publicly declared that his only hope in the recovery and development of the imbecile's mind rested with the patron. His earnest, simple faith in the ultimate cure of the child was impressive.

Brother André received the father and son in private. He talked with the parent for about a quarter of an hour. When the father and child walked out of the room the face of the former was radiant with joy. The boy seemed calm. Little tears stole down the cheeks of the parent as he looked at his offspring. They walk through a wondering crowd in the direction of the Crypt. Whether the child showed any improvement or not later, could not be ascertained because the father declined to reveal his name.

The line of people that sought a few words of advice from Brother André seemed unending. A feature that I considered interesting and important was the fact that there were as many or more men in the line as there were women. All displayed the same faith in the patron. It was the same all day. They came, talked with the pious old religious and went away to pray better for their visit.

As the hands on the great clock that hangs on the wall indicated that it was nearly four o'clock, the hour for Benediction, the little groups inside the shed began to break up. In twos and threes the people headed for the Crypt. Quickly the shed was deserted, except for Brother André and the little old French woman who sells the refreshments. He seemed slightly exhausted and visibly affected by the suffering he had witnessed and retired to his office for a few minutes before going over to the church.

Almost every seat in the Crypt was occupied when Brother André made his way out to the altar. He walked to one side where there was a kneeling bench and made the sign of the cross and immediately started to pray, his eyes riveted on the great statue of the patron. The majority of the people were already on their knees.

An Impressive Service

The catacomb-like structure was silent as the altar boys moved about before the shrine like fireflies. Each held a lighted taper in his hand and reverently went about his business of lighting the clusters of candles held in massive brass fixtures on and above the altar. The sweeping Byzantine arches hang low across the Crypt and seemed to make the silence oppressive.

Here and there pilgrims could be seen kneeling before the side altars. They made a strange picture. About them the multi-colored lights twinkled and spluttered revealing in their uncertain glow hundreds of crutches and other implements of the afflicted that bear mute testimony of the powers and goodness of the patron of the Oratory. The wavering lights danced about those symbols of infirmity with apparent joy for they represented the fruits of an all powerful faith.

While the preparations for Benediction are going on, sober brothers in their black cassocks move silently about the rear of the church assisting the people in every way. Frequently they stop to answer the inquiry of a worshiper or one drawn to the scene by curiosity. These kindly servants of God, humble and ever ready to assist the pilgrims in any way, give what assistance they can. The faithful flow in steady streams about them as the preparations for the afternoon service continue. Several of the brothers retire to the choir loft to lift their voices in adoration when the service starts. Others kneel humbly on the bare floor in the rear of the Crypt.

The mellow light of the declining sun filters

through the stained glass windows and is reflected on the great brass candlesticks on the main altar. Suddenly, the great clusters of electric lights above the altar are switched on. They are for the most part cleverly concealed and as they blaze forth, the statue of the patron is clearly revealed. The congregation, restless because of the silence is immediately all attention and all eyes are focused on the giant statue of Saint Joseph above the high altar.

There is a stir. The first of the altar boys has appeared, each carrying a candle in a large holder. They are lead by a large youth proudly carrying a cross. Behind them come the priests. Immediately the organ begins to thunder forth in tones familiar to Catholics the world over. Three priests of the household enter the sanctuary behind the acolytes. The deep voice of the organ becomes louder. It echoes and reverberates through the Crypt, the sounds seeming to gain in volume as they roll toward the front of the church. Soon the chanting voices of the brothers of the Order who make up the choir are heard.

The piety, sincerity and attention of the congregation is remarkable. All eyes are either on the great Carrara image of the humble carpenter of Nazareth over the main altar

or on the golden Monstrance in front of it
that contains the Sacred Host.

The most solemn moment in the service
arrives quickly—the elevation of the Monstrance—and the Benediction. The very air
in the vaulted spaces seems charged as the
pious petitions of the congregation rise to
Heaven. The Host is returned to the taber-
nacle and the peals of the organ once more fill
the Crypt. Many of the people leave the
church immediately. Others push their way
toward the altar where two priests carrying
the Sacred Relics of Saint Joseph have appeared.

The altar rail is quickly filled and the priests
with the relics in golden cases walk along it.
Most of the supplicants simply kiss the relic.
Others indicating parts of their afflicted bodies
have the priest apply the relic to them. After
the application of the relic most of the pilgrims retire to seats in the front of the church
and continue their prayers while the waves of
the earnest faithful continue to come forward
from the body of the church.

While the relics are being thus applied, off
in a quiet corner of the sanctuary unseen by
the throngs is Brother André imploring the
aid of the Mighty Protector of the Holy
Family for those who have come to do him

honor. He remains to pray a while after the last of the pilgrims have departed.

The shadows of night seem to fall quickly over Mount Royal. The Crypt is darkened except for the little dancing colored tapers and candles that have been lighted by the throng of the day. The place is deserted and silent except that here and there on the long flight of steps leading to the shrine can be seen straggling pilgrims who were unable for various reasons, to attend the afternoon services. Two of them are women evidently from their dress and poise from different stratas of society. Totally unconscious of what is going on about them they are quietly saying their beads as they pause momentarily and kneel on each step.

In the darkened church there are only a few. One youth on crutches is approaching the image of the patron on one of the side altars. With difficulty he reaches the kneeling bench and stands his crutches beside it. He looks pleadingly and longingly at the statue and begins to pray. In front of him he sees the crutches and canes of others who have come before him to pray and who have gone away cured. He prays long and earnestly and goes away filled with a hope that he never had before.

I called on Brother André after dinner. The pious old man himself opened the door and greeted me with a firm, friendly hand-clasp. His simple courtesy immediately impressed itself. He led the way into a plainly furnished reception room and insisted on returning to the hall to place my hat out of the way. I started to apologize for calling so late and inquired if he were not fatigued from the long day, explaining that I had observed the crowds of people he had talked with.

"Yes, many come to me today," he replied, "but I must talk with them. You are an American and I see many Americans today among the people. I have so many friends in the United States and I like them very much. Many of them have great devotion to Saint Joseph and all during the year they send letters to me telling of the blessings he has given them. They are a good people."

At the mention of the name of the patron Brother André's eyes brightened and he eagerly inquired if I had seen the Crypt and the large statue. I explained I had been in the church and thought I had seen everything there. Then he invited me to go over to the church so that he could show me the shrine. I protested that he was worn out from the efforts of the day. He only smiled and directed me to follow him.

On the way down the covered stone steps from the rectory to the church, I inquired my host's age. "I am very young," he replied. "I am only seven and six. That is thirteen." He laughed at his little joke which I afterward learned was one of his favorites. He certainly does not act or look to be seventy-six years old.

In the sacristy Brother André opened great closets revealing the beautiful vestments of the priests which were made especially for the Oratory. The room is spacious and well lighted and contains like almost every room about the Oratory an image of Saint Joseph.

Brother André turned on a couple of switches flooding the Crypt with light. Its massive bulk seemed to be even more impressive under the artificial glow. The towering statue of Saint Joseph which is over nine feet in height set in the center of the white marble altar seemed even larger from the back of the altar. He took great pride in explaining just how the hundreds of lights were arranged so that the imposing image would stand out the better.

Then he pointed out the scheme carried out in the stained glass windows, most all of which relate to the patron. The large window directly over the altar reveals him with a background of lilies. In his arms he holds the Child Jesus. The windows on either side are dedicated to the two other members of the Holy Family and are excellent works of art. One represents the Sacred Heart of Jesus and the other the Sacred Heart of Mary. The windows on the side of the Crypt depict the great events in the life of the humble carpenter of Nazareth. Brother André is rightly proud of these artistic reminders of his patron.

He pointed to the many images of Saint Joseph about the Crypt. He is especially pleased at the great number of colored tapers that flicker before them. A small crowned statue on the gospel side of the sanctuary, where numerous tapers burn, is of special interest. The lights are constantly burned for the host of subscribers to the *Annals* of the Oratory.

The confessionals and the furniture of the Crypt are all in natural wood. While the furniture is plain it is substantial and attractive. The Crypt as a whole is a most satisfying place of worship.

Brother André insisted on climbing into the belfry tower that I might see his special place of worship, the tiny chapel that is described elsewhere in this narrative. Then he went out in the rear. The workmen are blasting their way through the solid rock of Mount Royal for the foundation for the Basilica of Saint Joseph. This great basilica once only a far off dream of Brother André will be completed in about 1929 and will be one of the greatest edifices of its kind in the world.

As Brother André stood hatless in the moonlight on the rock, the wind whipping his cassock about him, he presented a picturesque figure. With enthusiasm he explained that the basilica will be built in the form of a cross and will have a great tower that will be visible from the river and the surrounding country. I must have been very silent when he was telling me of how his dream of erecting this great shrine to his patron will come true. He suddenly turned to me as if reading my thoughts and said:

"Yes, I will live to see it all completed."

We walked back to the rectory and on the way he spoke of his contemplated short vacation in New England. He said that his physicians now insist that he take two vacations a year, one in the spring and another in the fall. He always returns to those New England hills, the scenes of his early struggles, to rest that he may continue to carry on his mission in life—spreading the devotion of Saint Joseph.

Back in the rectory Brother André showed me the blueprints of the new basilica. For a man who can neither read nor write he certainly displayed a remarkable knowledge of the drawings. He said that many changes had been made in the original plans before they were acceptable to the authorities at the Oratory. The funds for the erection of the vast basilica which will cost well over two million dollars have been contributed and are still being contributed by those who have won health, happiness and better understanding on the rocks of Mount Royal.

Brother André inquired eagerly if I had visited his little chapel to the right of the rectory where he first met the pilgrims. That little flimsy, tin roofed chapel means much to the saintly old religious. He speaks of it with genuine affection. I observed that the great statue of the patron in the Crypt was more beautiful than the rather commonplace representation in the chapel. He agreed but said that he thought much of the old statue. He said that once while he was aiding a workman to move the statue, which is very heavy, that the man fell and that he was able to hold it alone although never before nor after could he do this.

As I was leaving I asked Brother André if he did not have some message for the American people he would like me to convey. He said:

"The United States is a great country and the people are very good. I would like to see even more of them with devotion to Saint Joseph. The patron would be pleased and he will protect and reward them."

At the door with a dignified motion of benediction this great servant of God with a hearty handclasp said; "Good night and God bless you and all the other Americans."

I walked down the sweeping road with a strange feeling. Brother André had made a profound impression on me. His simple faith and confidence in his patron was absolute. He is, indeed, a modern crusader and his only asset with which he has builded this great shrine besides his faith is prayer to his patron.

IV

What Is a Miracle?

WHEN assailants of Christianity launch an attack upon religion, they invariably focus their fire on the Roman Catholic Church. The first charge hurled is that it is a political monster that seeks to usurp governmental powers and that its millions of communicants are welded together only through "superstition." Through the ages that Christianity has successfully combated her enemies the one outstanding object of the anti-religionists has been concerted attempts to make supernatural manifestations look ridiculous.

The Catholic Church is especially selected as an object of attack by those opposed to religion because of their knowledge that if it falls all others will topple with it. Let us see the reason.

It is a well known and well established fact that the Catholic Church was founded on and rests on miracles. The Founder Himself, was the first and greatest miracle. His entire life from the time of His birth to His resurrection was simply a succession of miracles. If these miracles could be proven false and fraudulent, then Jesus Christ would be pronounced the greatest fraud the world had ever known and the church he founded would quickly crumble and decay. The religion which has endured through twenty centuries of the bitterest of persecution would be proven a fraud. In such an event Catholicity would quickly disappear and with it all religion and man would be free to give full rein to the passions that have only been held in restraint during the ages by religion. Such is the logic of the anti-religion-ists and it is correct, for if the Catholic Church falls none other can survive.

In the beginning of Protestantism in the drift toward rationalism and infidelity it became necessary for the opponents of the Church to deny the miraculous. Their initial denials were confined to the later day miracles. They willingly admitted the possibility of the miracles recorded in the gospels upon which Christianity rests. This reasoning which prompted them to accept the miracles of the remote past and to flatly deny those of later ages rapidly became a source of embarrassment to them. The inconsistency of this position taken by those who broke away from the Church finally forced their followers to reject miracles as a whole. They could not admit supernatural intervention during one period and deny it during another. To accept miracles during modern times would mean at least tentative recognition of the only church in which they were wrought, the Roman Catholic. Rather than do this the leaders of Protestant thought rejected all miracles and thus we find today that belief in the miraculous is dead outside the Catholic Church.

The general attitude outside the Church today is that miracles are simply impossible. The very idea that they could occur in this enlightened age is not acceptable and is really offensive to the so called leaders in modern thought. They are unbelievers, firm in their convictions and emphatically decline to listen to the evidence nor will they delve into or investigate miracles in the same way they do other things in a scientific way. If they would do this they might find in an honest inquiry, fairly conducted, abundant proof of the fallacy of their position. Further they would find that the Catholic Church which has fostered science through the centuries does not clash with science in the matter of miracles.

If they are right in their theories and beliefs, Jesus Christ was a fraud. If his whole life was not a series of miracles when he gave sight to the blind, cleansed the lepers, raised the dead, calmed the elements and finally rose from the dead Himself, then the Catholic Church which he founded is the biggest fraud of all times. If the Catholic Church was not founded upon miracles, if its millions of martyrs died because of fraudulent miracles, then its triumphant progress through twenty centuries of persecution and assault constitutes an even greater miracle than any that has been claimed for it. If the whole structure of this far reaching, powerful organization has been builded upon fraud it should be destroyed and the quicker the better for humanity.

What does the Catholic Church mean by a miracle? Simply this. When the Church refers to a miracle it means some visible action or occurrence that is far above the laws and powers of nature. Since only the Almighty Himself is capable of interfering with the laws of nature the performance of a miracle must be accepted as evidence of God's activity in a special or unusual way.

A miracle is really an occurrence that takes place in violation of the laws of nature and cannot be accounted for except by the admission of supernatural intervention. It is a sign of the connection between the supernatural world and ours. Miracles are not performed by the Heavenly powers to repair any defect in the scheme of nature as we know it but in answer to the prayers and petitions of suffering humanity.

When Catholics raise their voices in prayer they do not intercede with God to perform miracles in their behalf. When they prostrate themselves at a shrine they do not ask nor expect that a miracle will be the answer to their prayers. They simply intercede with Him trusting that in His infinite wisdom and power he will bring about what they ask if it is for His honor and glory.

It is the miracles of the present age that we are most concerned with now. Do they really occur? Is there not some trick or magic behind them? If you think so a visit to Saint Joseph's Oratory, Lourdes, or any of the great shrine centers of devotion will convince you. Unprejudiced persons on investigation are quickly convinced that the facts as presented by the authorities are authentic. The facts that cures of an extraordinary nature have been recorded are frankly admitted by scientists and medical men who are unbelievers. They do not admit the supernatural, it is true, but explain the cures by occult forces. They claim the pilgrim is swept away by the exaltation of the spirit in the midst of such piety and devotion that prevails at the shrines and that this reacts on the body as a stimulus and effects what seems to be a cure.

This is a material age that depends upon material evidence. Science has made great progress, especially the science of medicine. Therefore in the succeeding chapter are submitted a series of cures that have withstood the most rigorous inquiry from every angle. The theory that the miracles of one generation are the scientific facts of the next has not held in these cases. The records of authentication are on file at the Oratory of Saint Joseph, where they may be examined and the vast majority of those mentioned are also alive and are always willing and happy to verify the cures.

V

Cures

The Cure of Arthur Rochette

EARLY in 1912, Arthur Rochette was in the employ of the Grand Trunk Railway, at Richmond, Quebec, in the capacity of a brakeman. In the course of his regular work on a freight train he slipped on the rails and was hurled beneath a train, two wheels passing over his right foot and left ankle. He was rescued from further injury by fellow workmen and the first medical aid was given him by Dr. Hayes, a surgeon in the employ of the railway. The diagnoses of this medical man was "Crushing of both feet, especially the left; compound fracture of bones of left foot, followed by infection."

The injured man was rushed to the General Hospital at Montreal. There he was given expert treatment and the right foot quickly responded to it and healed. The efforts to heal the left foot were not so successful and

it became gangrenous. This condition resulted in two operations to save the foot.
After the second operation the patient took a
turn for the worse and blood poisoning set in
and amputation seemed almost inevitable.
The surgeons suggested a third operation
which would result in the removal of the
ailing member. Rochette, flatly refused to
permit this and asked that his father be sent
for. At the urging of the son, his father had
him removed from the hospital.

He apparently left the hospital in worse
condition than when he entered it a month
before. He was going home to die because of
his refusal to follow the advice of the eminent
surgeons who had examined him and who had
advocated another operation. His foot just
dangled from his leg, being held on only by
the skin and tissue, the bones being broken.
The muscles were crushed into the bone and
although the pain was terrific he would turn
his foot more than halfway around without
difficulty. The poisonous inflammation set
in quickly and the foot and leg swelled to
three times their normal size. His immediate
family being alarmed, called in the parish
priest and the sufferer was given the last
sacraments in preparation for death. Hope
was almost abandoned and the poor neighbors

of the farmer Rochette, at Princeville, hourly expected to hear of the passing of their friend.

One day Mr. Arthur Gilbert, the member of the Federal Parliament from the district, called to see the dying youth who was his neighbor. The legislator talked with the youth and suggested that he ask the intervention of Saint Joseph to relieve his sufferings. At the same time he counselled him to communicate with Brother André at Saint Joseph's Oratory. The family were devout Catholics of French origin and eagerly followed the suggestion of Mr. Gilbert.

They wrote to Brother André and a few days later an answering missive was received from him that carried a message of hope and faith into the sick room. Brother André had sent along a small phial of holy oil and a medal of Saint Joseph which he urged should be applied to the injured limb. They were and immediate relief was felt. The patient and members of his family joined in novenas to the mighty patron. They were sure that Saint Joseph would effect a cure in the case and confidently waited. The fear of death passed and the swelling disappeared. The improvement of the patient was steady. Within a week he was able to sit up in bed. His strength seemed to return rapidly and soon he was able to go out with the aid of crutches. His foot still was useless and could not bear his weight. Because of this condition he was forced to have a local shoemaker construct a special boot for him. Neighbors who knew of the severe attack of blood poisoning he had suffered marveled at his recovery which they attributed to supernatural intervention.

He communicated with Brother André and told him of the circumstances of the cure. Four months later he decided to invade Saint Joseph's haven of devotion on Mount Royal and implore a complete cure. Before starting on the journey he again had his foot examined by two physicians who had previously treated him. They found that although the swelling had gone down and the evidences of blood poisoning had disappeared, the foot still swung helplessly from the leg. On the leg they noted seven gaping wounds which were open. From these there was an offensive odor and the flesh about them had lost its sense of touch.

The surgeons when informed of his mission failed to enthuse. One strongly urged that he immediately submit to an operation that would mean amputation of the leg. This he refused to do. The other doctor branded the case as hopeless without an operation and voiced the opinion that whoever could cure the brakeman's leg could just as easily take a large church and turn it end on end.

At the Oratory he met and talked with Brother André who approved of his determination not to submit to an operation. He remained to finish the novena and then returned to Richmond filled with a great hope but not cured. He, however, ceased taking medical treatment and following the advice of the saintly Brother simply washed the wounds daily with warm water and applied the oil of Saint Joseph. According to the best knowledge of medicine this treatment should have brought on the gangrene but to the amazement of everyone the foot continued to improve.

A month later he made another pilgrimage to the Oratory and made a novena of Communions. At the conclusion of this he had improved so that he wanted to leave his crutches at the shrine but Brother André persuaded him not to do so. A few weeks later he put aside his crutches for good. He was completely cured.

The surgeons who two months previously had informed him that an operation only would save his life could not account for the cure. They refused to admit that the cure was even extraordinary and refused to submit authenticating documents. However, there is abundant material of this nature from Mr. Gilbert, the Rochette family, and neighbors on file at the Oratory. Rochette is still (1924) in the very best of health and has never been given the least trouble by the badly mangled foot that once threatened his life so seriously.

Mlle. Marie-Antoinette Mercier

One of the most amazing cures recorded through intercession to Saint Joseph since the founding of the inspiring Oratory on the flank of Mount Royal was that of Mlle. Marie-Antoinette Mercier, a student at St. Joseph's Convent, at Levis, just across the great river from the City of Quebec. This cure was fully observed and authenticated by distinguished physicians who were able to speak of it with real authority. It was a cure of the type that cannot be denied, it was indeed, a supernatural manifestation of the powers of the mighty patron and the reward of earnest prayer. The facts are these.

On a summer morning in 1909, Mlle. Marie Mercier was playing on a lake with some friends from her convent school. A companion struck her a cruel blow in the right eye with an oar. The injury proved severe

and oculists called to attend her made frantic
efforts to save the sight of the eye. Their
efforts were futile and paralysis of the optic
nerve set in. The case seemed hopeless.
The girl student returned to her classes but
because of her misfortune could take little
part in the work of the students. The nuns
were heartbroken that such an accident should
overtake one entrusted to their care.

They had heard stories of the wonders
worked at the Oratory of Saint Joseph, at
Montreal and of Brother André the pious old
apostle of faith who presided over the Oratory.
They were much impressed and according to
the dictates of the cloistered life they decided
that an appeal to Heaven would be fitting
and proper under the circumstances. They
decided to start a novena to the patron of
the Convent and asked that the students join
in their prayers for the recovery of their
stricken classmate. They obtained a medal
that had been blessed at the Oratory.

For eight days everyone in the Convent received daily Communion and the injured
child with the utmost confidence in Saint
Joseph applied the medal to her injured eye.
During that period there was no improvement
she could notice. However, she did not aban-
don hope, for the novena lasted nine days.

On the ninth day after the whole community had approached the altar and received the Host she suddenly noticed that with the eye that had been paralyzed she could see the statue of Saint Joseph. She had been unable to observe it from the time of her injury. Mlle. Mercier was almost overcome at the sight. In her joy she exclaimed "I see," and buried her head in her hands to offer a hasty thanksgiving. Those about her heard the cry and a wave of gratitude and deep emotion swept the chapel. The holy sisters and students could hardly wait for the completion of the Mass. When it was over they crowded about her and showered her with congratulations that she had been especially selected by the mighty Foster Father of Jesus for a manifestation of his powers and goodness.

Once outside the chapel the sisters, convinced of the miraculous cure that had taken place in their midst were anxious to verify it. They produced a book printed with exceptionally small type and asked the child to read it which she did without difficulty. She did not hesitate at her task nor feel any fatigue when she completed it. The sisters and students were deeply impressed and immediately in unison started singing a canticle of the Deeds of Grace. The girl student herself

ORATORY OF SAINT JOSEPH

How the mighty Citadel of Faith in Honor of Saint Joseph will look when completed

was almost overcome that such a great grace should be showered down upon her. Her relatives on hearing the glad news dropped on their knees to offer thanks to Saint Joseph for his wonderful favor.

Dr. L. O. Gauthier, of Quebec, attended the girl when she was first injured. On June 19, 1909, he issued the following certificate on the condition of the student:

"I, the undersigned, Medical Doctor and Oculist, certify that I have been attending Mlle. Marie-Antoinette Mercier for an injury to her right eye, a severe traumatism which will probably involve the loss of that eye through atrophy of the optic nerve. I may add my opinion that, if the girl had at once been taken to a specialist, the accident might have had less serious results and that the oculist might have prevented the complete atrophy of the nerve.

"In testimony whereof I subscribe myself,

"DR. L. O. GAUTHIER."

After the cure of Mlle. Mercier she was again given a thorough examination by Dr. Gauthier. Under the date of February 10, 1910, issuing a certificate he wrote:

"I, the undersigned, a Medical Doctor and Oculist certify that on June 3, 1909, I examined

Marie Antoinette for an accident to her right eye, and found that the eye was in an amaurotic condition, that its sight was lost. I also diagnosed hemorrhages in connection with the optic nerve, tending to bring about blindness by compression.

"Today, February 15, 1910, I have again examined Mlle. Mercier and find that the sight of her right eye is about normal, a circumstance which would indicate that a complete revolution of the nerve has taken place. I am not prepared to admit that the sight of this eye has been restored through purely natural means.

"In testimony whereof, I subscribe myself,

"DR. L. O. GAUTHIER."

Additional testimony of an authenticating nature was given by Dr. Wilfred Beaupré who was more positive in his conclusion that supernatural intervention had saved the sight of Mlle. Mercier. On September 15, 1909, at his office in Quebec he wrote:

"I, the undersigned certify that on June 19th last, I examined the eyesight of Mlle. Marie-Antoinette Mercier, residing at No. 20 Laval St., and found that the sight of her right eye was absolutely null. She told me that she had received a traumatism on this eye a fortnight earlier, and attributed the loss of its sight to the blow she had received.

"DR. WILF. BEAUPRÉ."

Five months later after the reported cure of
Mlle. Mercier following the novena to St.
Joseph, Dr. Beaupré again gave her a thorough
examination. Of this under date of February
15, 1910, he had this to say:

"On June 19th, 1909, I examined at my office
with all due care, the eyesight of Mlle. Marie-
Antoinette Mercier, thirteen years of age and residing at No. 20 Laval St., Quebec. Her mother
who accompanied her, told me that the girl had
received a fortnight before, full on the right eye,
a blow from an oar in the hands of a little girl who,
apparently, was somewhat malicious; and that,
since then, her daughter had lost the sight of that
eye.

"An external examination of the eye disclosed
nothing unusual and absolutely no trace of traumatism. The examination of the interior of the
eye, made with an ophthalmoscope, was rendered
almost impossible on account of a considerable
disturbance of the vitreous humor. There was, I
think, evidence of hemorrhages. I must admit,
however, that on this first examination I was unable to make an absolutely precise diagnosis.

"Pursuing my examination I found that no
luminous perception existed in the eye, and that
it was completely impervious to light. This was
a very serious matter, for it argued the probability
of the optic nerves' being already in a more or less
advanced stage of atrophy.

"I had no hesitation, accordingly, in assuring the mother that the eye would eventually be lost, and that no human means could bring back its sight. Such was my sincere conviction. At the same time I told the mother that if the child were mine I would have her undergo a 'new' treatment which had already produced successful results in certain ocular troubles. The mother decided that the treatment in question should be given, and accordingly during some weeks the girl was submitted to this 'special treatment' but without the slightest result, as was proved by the examination of the eye on August 26, 1909. I then advised that it be discontinued. I have forgotten to state that on the occasion of their first visit to me on June 19th, the mother asked me whether it would not be well to operate on the injured eye, or even take it out to better protect the other eye. I told her that in my opinion there would be no need of operating, and no danger of the left eye being affected.

"On August 26th, the girl and her father came to see me, and the latter asked me to make another examination and to give him a certificate attesting that the right eye would remain useless, if that were my opinion, because he told me he intended suing for damages and would need such a certificate. I made the examination, which served only to strengthen my conviction as to the total and permanent loss of the eye's sight.

"On the ninth of February, 1910, Mlle. Mercier

again came to my office for a new consultation.
The religious who accompanied her, the Reverend
Mother St. Ephrem of St. Joseph's Convent at
Levis, informed me to my astonishment that Marie
Antoinette Mercier who, that very morning, had
finished a novena to St. Joseph, had suddenly during Mass recovered her sight. I made, not without considerable emotion another examination of
her right eye, and found that for the first time I
could see into the depths of the eye, and that,
moreover, the sight of the eye was absolutely perfect and in every respect equal to that of the left
eye, which was perfectly normal.

"It is needless to dwell upon my astonishment or
on the girl's happiness. If the finger of God is not
manifest in this cure, then I do not know whose
finger has been working.

"W. Beaupré, M. D."

A Protestant Beneficiary Who Did Not Believe in Miracles

The beneficiary of one of the most remarkable cures recorded and authenticated at the
Oratory was that of an English Protestant
fireman in the city of Westmount, just outside of Montreal. The man's name is Alfred
Standhope who before the events of 1917 was
a typical skeptic who sneered at the possibility
of miracles in this great twentieth century.
His story briefly is this.

In April of 1916 he was engaged in his regular occupation as a fireman in the Westmount brigade. On the fifth of the month he was in the sitting room on the second floor of the fire house when he attempted to descend to the ground floor as is done by firemen the world over by means of a brass pole. He lost his grip on the pole and was hurled to the cement floor thirty feet below. Comrades rushed to his aid and found that his feet were badly injured and that his shattered thigh bone protruded through the skin. He was taken to the Western Hospital. There he received treatment for six weeks.

He was discharged with a bad infection in one of his feet which caused much suppuration, and terrible suffering whenever he attempted the slightest task. His hope of complete recovery seemed remote. Most of his fellow firemen were French-Canadians who poured out their sympathy to him. Several urged that he visit the great shrine of Saint Joseph on the flank of Mount Royal and talk with Brother André. In the beginning he resented the idea. Then when they continued to urge he decided to at least try intercession to St. Joseph as his suffering was intense.

Early in June, 1917, he made his way up the tortuous path of the afflicted that leads to the little office of Brother André. The aged religious received him with great sympathy and listened to his tale of misfortune. He removed his shoe and stocking from the ailing foot and Brother André laid his hand on the injured member. Standhope declares that at the touch of the saintly character of Mount Royal the terrible pain he had known for months disappeared never to return. His foot and leg seemed to recover their old-time vigor and he walked away after murmuring a word of thanksgiving to St. Joseph and Brother André.

Standhope was forced to leave the Westmount Fire Brigade because of his injury. He is now employed and has been since 1917, after his visit to Brother André, as a night watchman for the Imperial Tobacco Company. In this capacity he is compelled to make three rounds of the extensive establishment every night and to fire two large furnaces. Not once since his visit to Brother André has his foot given him the slightest trouble, according to his testimony.

He has never visited Brother André nor the Oratory since the day of his recovery but needless to say he is deeply appreciative for the recovery of his health. Mr. Standhope is a powerful, heavy set and very silent man especially when he is talking about his recovery.

However, he is always happy to express his gratitude for the extraordinary grace that came to him.

Since the creation of the Oratory there have been numerous specific cures, especially in cases of cancer and tuberculosis which have been authenticated that are well worth mentioning. One of note was that of Mr. J. O. Dufresne, of Nicolet, Quebec, which took place late in 1911. Mr. Dufresne was a victim of tuberculosis and during the course of the disease his brother Dr. G. A. Henri Dufresne made frantic efforts to cure his brother or at least check the ravages of the disease. His efforts proved futile. He made a pilgrimage to the Oratory and at the completion of his novena to Saint Joseph he was cured. In writing of this cure to the Provincial of the Congregation of the Holy Cross in charge of the Oratory, Dr. Dufresne said:

"I, the undersigned, testify that Mr. J. O. Dufresne, of Nicolet, has been cured of tuberculosis in a very far advanced stage after a pilgrimage to the Oratory of St. Joseph on Mount Royal.

"I attended the patient before his pilgrimage and then believed that his death was imminent. A year has elapsed since his cure took place, and it still persists,

" (Signed) G. A. DUFRESNE, M.D."

It is interesting to note that another tubercular patient who had been under the care of Dr. Dufresne was also a beneficiary of the goodness of St. Joseph after intercession at the Oratory. His certificate of authentication which is on file at the shrine is self explanatory. It reads:

"I, the undersigned, certify that during the four years prior to the month of May, 1910, I was attendant physician to Mlle. Alphonsine Saint Martin, and considered her at the date mentioned a victim of tuberculosis in the secondary stage.

"Since that time she has become completely well and her lungs are sound. I satisfied myself as to this amelioration on her return from a pilgrimage which she made to the Oratory of St. Joseph in May, 1910.

"(Signed)

"G. A. DUFRESNE, M.D."

Both these certifications are on file at the Oratory and may be examined. Twelve years later when this is written according to the best available information the cures still persist and the former victims of the great "white plague" are enjoying the very best of health. Another cure of the same type which has been authenticated at the Oratory is that of Charles Eugene Veilleux, of River du Loup which took place during 1911. The medical certificate filed says:

"I, the undersigned, medical practitioner at Fraserville, certify, that in company with Dr. F. E. Gilbert, I examined young Veilleux, son of Mr. Eugene Veilleux of this place about August 30, 1910. We found that the youth was suffering from tuberculosis of the spinal column, in the cervical region. We put him in a plaster cast. Several weeks later the boy went to Montreal with his mother and came back completely cured. On different occasions since then I have examined the boy and have never been able to discover the slightest trace of the terrible disease from which he had suffered, a disease the treatment for which usually takes more than three years.

" (Signed)

"L. J. PIUZE, M.D."

The Cure of Mdme. Joseph Marcoux

Mdme. Marcoux was a victim of a serious heart affliction which threatened at any moment to snuff out the remaining spark of life in her body. She was weak and constantly in dread of what was to come. Early in the summer of 1921, Brother André was visiting the headquarters of the Congregation of the

Holy Cross, in St. Famille St., Quebec. Mons. Marcoux hearing of the visit of the pious porter of Cotes Des Neiges hastened to ask his aid. He asked Brother André to come to his home and see his wife whom he deeply loved. While he was talking with the old religious, a sudden change for the better came over his wife and when he returned to the house with Brother André he was astounded to find her sitting up in a room other than her bedroom apparently in good health. Brother André breathed his usual message of faith into the ears of the happy woman. He told her to invoke the aid of Saint Joseph in her prayers and suggested that she always have on hand some of the holy oil and that she wear a medallion of the patron. She did all these things and under date of June 25th, 1921, her attending physician, Dr. M. A. Falardeau of Quebec, in attesting to her cure wrote:

"I, the undersigned, solemnly declare that Mdme. Joseph Marcoux, of No. 76 Lachevrotiere Street, Quebec, has been under my care since December 27, 1920; that she had been suffering a very severe form of heart disease, her limbs inflamed, and of such pronounced weakness that I considered it a desperate case.

"Now, she is well, her heart beats normally, her pulse is good and her limbs are in normal condition.

I consider that this is a wonderful grace obtained
by Brother André, of Saint Joseph's Oratory,
Montreal."

Crutches Discarded

Joseph L'Heureux, the son of Mons. L'Heureux, of Messrs. L'Heureux & Gauvin, of
Quebec, was a sufferer from a severe bone
disease of the hip for six years. For over a
year he had been forced to get about with the
aid of crutches. In 1910, he made a novena to
Saint Joseph at the Oratory and at the conclusion of which he discarded his crutches and
walked away without their aid, cured. His
implements of misfortune and suffering were
added to the growing pile at the Oratory that
testify mutely to the goodness of the all powerful patron of the shrine.

The father of this boy especially selected
for extraordinary grace in a letter to the Oratory verifying the cure under date of October
13, 1910, wrote:

"With regard to the cure of my son, here is the
note which I have caused to be published in the
Quebec newspapers:

" 'Young Joseph L'Heureux, fifteen years of age,
son of Mons. L'Heureux, of Messrs. L'Heureux and
Gauvin, had suffered for six years from a bone

disease, and for more than a year had been forced
to walk on crutches. A novena which was begun
in Quebec and terminated at the Oratory of St.
Joseph of the Mountain, Cotes Des Neiges, ·
Montreal, obtained for him a perfect cure inso-
much that the patient left his crutches at the
Oratory.' Mr. L'Heureux himself has asked us to
bring this to public attention in order to spread
the cult of devotion to the foster father of the
Savior, Jesus Christ. With everlasting gratitude.
" (Signed)

"EHPREM L'HEUREUX,

"No. 391 St. Joseph St., Quebec."

It is the custom of the authorities of the
Oratory to verify the cures recorded after a
period has passed. In 1922, following this
custom they wrote to ascertain whether the
cure still prevailed. The father of the boy
and his physician had long since passed to
their reward when the inquiry arrived and it
was answered in person by the beneficiary of
the grace. His verification letter read:

"For upwards of two years I had to walk with
the aid of crutches, and was unable to use my right
leg. Then, having heard of the wonderful miracles
performed by St. Joseph, through the intercession
of Brother André, I made a novena to St. Joseph,
in the hope of obtaining a cure of my malady.

"At the conclusion of the novena I went to Montreal to see Brother André. On arrival there I had a talk with him, and told him that I had the utmost confidence in his prayers to his patron, Saint Joseph. At that same instant I allowed my crutches to drop to the ground, just as I walk today without difficulty. And I assure you Monsieur, that from that time until now I have never suffered from any hip disease. I carry myself very well today, just as on the day when I was first cured."

When this enlightening and interesting document arrived the priests at the Oratory were deeply impressed and made efforts to obtain medical certificates. However, they were unable to do this because the physicians who attended L'Heureux and his father had passed on to their reward. The records as stated above are on file at the Oratory and can be examined by anyone.

Mr. Louis Bertrand

In the case of Mons. Bertrand there is presented a perfect and permanent cure of a serious malady which had defied the experts of medical science. For three years Mr. Louis Bertrand had suffered from a cancer on the right arm as attested to by numerous distinguished physicians who had examined him. The case to them seemed hopeless. They had done all in their power and there was no sign of improvement. The best way to present the case would be to let the attending physicians tell the tale of his suffering as they did to the Oratory. As told by them it is as follows:

" MONTREAL, May 6th, 1911.

"Mr. Louis Bertrand, of No. 74a Saint Margaret St., St. Henri (on the outskirts of Montreal), was suffering from a cancer on the right arm. Already the ganglions of the axilla (armpit) and the arm had been attacked. The wound caused by the cancer increased in size rapidly, the cancerous infection making daily progress. I had not the slightest doubt as to the diagnosis of the case; it was really a cancer in the malignant stage.

"I certify that today, Mr. Bertrand is completely cured, that the ganglions have disappeared and that there is no trace of the cancerous infection. As Mr. Bertrand assures me that he has no recourse to medicial remedies—remedies which, for that matter, had previously proved ineffective, so his cure is certainly in effect a miracle, due to the intercession of Saint Joseph, in whom Mr. Bertrand placed his hope.

"DR. E. C. CAMPEAU, M.D.

"829 Notre Dame St., Montreal."

The cases thus far cited are typical of
thousands that have been recorded by the
authorities at the Oratory. Each month in
the official organ of the shrine, the *Annals*
there is published a list of between two and
three hundred "thanksgivings" from persons
who have received special graces during the
preceding month. This means that since
the creation of the Oratory as a special
place of devotion approximately thirty-five
thousand who have prostrated themselves
before the altar to ask special favors have had
their prayers answered.